The
Vine
and the
Branches

How to Spiritually Connect in a Challenging World

By Bryan Holmes and Maggie McSpedon

VITIS PRESS

Watertown

VITIS PRESS
A self-publishing enterprise in Watertown, Connecticut

The Vine and the Branches: How to Spiritually Connect in a Challenging World
Bryan Holmes and Maggie McSpedon

Copyeditor: Provided by CreateSpace, an Amazon Company
Interior Design: Bryan Holmes and Maggie McSpedon
Cover Design: Bryan Holmes, Maggie McSpedon, and CreateSpace Cover Creator

All profits from the sale of this book will go to charities that help enable spiritual connections.
Details are on Bryan Holmes's author website, including ways to help.

ISBN-13: 978-1494967543
ISBN-10: 1494967545

Library of Congress Control Number: 2014932661

Contents

Acknowledgments

We both want to thank many people for helping us review this book and improve it. Our families were very understanding as we wrote and worked on the project in the midst of our busy lives. They also provided many helpful comments and suggestions. Bryan's colleagues and friends were also very helpful, especially David, Liz, and Wes. Finally, Bryan's pastor, John, was an invaluable asset in ensuring the Bible passages and basic Christian doctrine were accurately portrayed.

Acknowledgm

Preface

Spirituality, the idea of being connected spiritually to God and to others, is a timeless concept in most cultures. People have felt that they have some sort of existence outside of their corporeal selves, and that they have a connection to those around them and to some sort of higher consciousness. Many have also understood that this spiritual life is eternal and should be the main focus while living on earth. However, life in today's world is mainly focused on bodily existence. To its detriment, modern society has neglected and negated spirituality. Many people now feel disconnected from one another and from any notion of a higher being or God. Until all of us begin to truly understand our spiritual selves and how we interconnect spiritually, we will be lost in our quest to solve society's problems or our own.

This book is an attempt to examine many of the social ills that plague society today, to analyze them, and to provide solutions in the context of spirituality. It is not a typical self-help book, but rather a call for self-examination and spiritual renewal through the help of other people and God. A major impetus for the book was the tragic shooting in December 2012 at Sandy Hook Elementary School in Newtown, Connecticut, less than twenty miles from where the authors live. As the news story unfolded over the past year, it became obvious that the shooter, Adam Lanza, had become isolated from society. Given the horrific nature of his crime, we cannot believe he felt any spiritual connection with God or with other people. Yet the news never mentioned anything concerning his spirituality. The story quickly devolved into a politically charged debate over gun control and mental health treatment. As terrible as this crime was, it was soon followed by other shootings and acts of violence. Our society was missing the true cause of all these crimes, and in so doing, was further promoting the lie that humankind can exist without spirituality.

On a positive note, the need for spirituality was very evident after the Newtown tragedy among the families of the victims, the survivors, first responders, and others in the community. Religious leaders of various faiths also served heroically to help these people. Many people gave moving testimony of their spiritual faith and how it helped them through this crisis. The spiritual connections they had were crucially important. Nevertheless, the mainstream media and other public commentators have never explicitly compared the demonstrated power of spiritual connections among these survivors to the spiritual vacuum of the perpetrator. While nobody knows exactly what Adam Lanza's spiritual state was at the time of his crime, his actions point to a complete absence of spiritual connections.

Historically, in many different cultures, spiritual disconnection, especially from God, has been identified as the source of evil and criminal behavior. The idea of Satan, an angel who transgressed against God, is the ultimate example of such disconnect. Despite this consistent view of evil and its source, we don't discuss it publicly through the media or in our social institutions. Why? It may be due to a misguided notion that any discussion of spirituality will somehow discriminate against one group or another. While the authors do not advocate for some sort of national spiritual policy, we do think that spirituality should be discussed openly in public forums. More importantly, each person must individually acknowledge his or her spiritual self and the need for spiritual connections with one another and with God. Until each of us does this, we will continue misdiagnosing the fundamental reasons for social calamities, and we will continue to struggle with them.

Many people feel driven to understand their spirituality. Albert Schweitzer, the theologian and missionary, wrote, "From the very beginning [of my youth] I was convinced that all thought is really concerned with the great problem of how man can attain to the spiritual union with infinite Being."[1] He felt compelled to understand the way he could spiritually connect with God. For any of us, the first step is self-examination. A placard reads, "Man know thyself," above an ancient church in Methwold, England. The point is that until a person looks within and makes an honest self-assessment, he or she cannot really understand his or her spiritual state. If this self-assessment shows a spiritual void, then the next step is to seek spiritual connection with God and with others. Every faith provides a way to do this.

Our main point in this book is that our modern world essentially promotes an existence lacking in any spirituality. Whatever spiritual connections we make are either ignored or attacked by the world around us. Insidiously, we have come to accept this state of being as normal. Historically, most cultures would consider it abnormal. We hope that in reading this book, you may discover normalcy, the existence of your spiritual self, and venture outside yourself to form spiritual connections. There is no single path to follow. With God's help and the support of those around you, you should tread the path best suited to you.

This book is the creation of two people, Bryan Holmes and Maggie McSpedon. Bryan was the instigator and primary author, and Maggie was a major contributor, content editor, creative consultant, and sounding-board. At every step of the way, we worked together, as we both share a similar view of spirituality. In places where only one of us is making a point, we put *Bryan* or *Maggie* at the beginning of the entry to indicate who is speaking, and we indicate the end of the entry using *~End~*. Otherwise, this book is the work of both of us.

While authored by Christians, this book in no way condemns other religions or beliefs. Rather, it affirms the existence of a common sense of spirituality among people of every faith. This book is also not promoting any particular form of politics or economics, but only offering criticism of the prevalent systems and indicating how they have hurt our spiritual existence. The fact that we are now in a new economic age, the information society[2], drives many of the social changes that cause enormous disruptions in our lives and severe fractures in our spirituality. Secular humanism and materialism are the fundamental philosophies of Western society that deny spirituality while guiding almost all major scholarly research and public discussion. Government-sponsored socialism in various forms is also a viable force in our global society and has had a hugely negative effect on spirituality. Finally, materialism and the economic force of our information society have accelerated globalization and urbanization, two major trends that stymie the development of our spiritual connections.

The evidence that these various political and economic systems have hurt the human condition is manifest, especially in the widespread discontent and violence we see around the world. Nevertheless, this book is not a call for political action to overthrow these systems. Instead, it is a call for each person to look within, acknowledge his or her need for spirituality, and begin to connect spiritually with others and with God. This is humanity's most important task. If every person made this effort, imagine the effect on every aspect of society.

One

Entangled and Connected

Understanding Spiritual Connections

The basic need for interaction is and always has been a part of human beings' nature. However, it is the effectiveness of these interactions that needs to be examined. *Spiritual connection* implies a religious aspect, but what is a "connection" and what does it entail? Is there any sort of connection we can measure or observe? There is a scientific basis for believing that all things, and therefore people, are linked, though the essence of these connections is still not fully understood.

Quantum physics shows that atomic particles can display a mysterious form of connection called *entanglement*. For instance, when two quantum entangled electrons are separated and the spin of one is altered, the other electron's spin will mirror the change, even though there is no measurable connection between them. Fritjof Capra, in *The Web of Life*, summarizes this revolution in scientific thought that quantum physics caused:

> The subatomic particles have no meaning as isolated entities but can be understood only as interconnections, or correlations, among various processes of observation and measurement. In other words, subatomic particles are not "things," but interconnections among things, and so on. In quantum theory we never end up with any "things;" we always deal with interconnections. This is how quantum physics shows that we cannot decompose the world into independently existing elementary units. As we shift our attention from macroscopic objects to atoms and subatomic particles, nature does not show us any isolated building blocks, but rather appears as a complex web of relationships among the various parts of a unified whole.[3]

We see that matter, at its most fundamental form, is connected. While the mechanics of this connection are unknown, the effects are observable. If matter, of which everything is made, is interconnected, would it be reasonable to assume this interconnectedness extends to things made of matter, including humans? We do not have good empirical proof of human interconnections, but we also lack a full comprehension of the human brain and the mind's relation to it.

Therefore, we must acknowledge the possibility that human connections occur in a realm that is currently outside our ability to observe it.

In *The Hidden Connections,* Capra explains that the word *spirit* has come down to us from many languages and cultures as meaning *breath of life.* [4] He suggests that the concept of spirituality can be explained by considering that all life is interconnected:

> Spirit—the breath of life—is what we have in common with all living beings. It nourishes us and keeps us alive...It is evident that this notion of spirituality is consistent with the notion of the embodied mind that is now being developed in cognitive science. Spiritual experience is an experience of aliveness of mind and body as a unity. Moreover, this experience of unity transcends not only the separation of mind and body, but also the separation of self and world. The central awareness in these spiritual moments is a profound sense of oneness with all, a sense of belonging to the universe as a whole. This sense of oneness with the natural world is fully borne out by the new scientific conception of life.[5]

We can also see how nature is interconnected in the study of ecology. Experience has taught us that when we affect our natural environment through pollution or species endangerment, severe consequences ensue. We are often surprised by the results of our actions, which frequently exhibit previously undiscovered connections. For instance, some species of large game fish, such as tuna, now contain dangerously high levels of mercury. Yet tuna do not consume mercury directly. They acquire it through the consumption of smaller fish, which consume the microorganisms that absorb mercury. This mercury is present in the water as a result of human wastes. This domino effect is a recurring theme in nature. Despite our vast research, there are millions of chain reactions still undiscovered in every facet of the environment.

The interconnections of the natural world are viewed spiritually by many faiths. In an introductory essay to the book, *Seeing God Everywhere: Essays on Nature and the Sacred (Perennial Philosophy)*, Satish Kumar describes the Hindu view, also shared by many other religions, "The god is not outside the world but the world is an embodiment of the divine. There is no separation, no division, no duality and no fragmentation. Everything is connected to everything else and the existence of one is dependent on the existence of the other."[6] All creation is connected to one another and to the Creator.

Bryan: I have felt this interconnection with nature many times as I have hiked in the mountains, swum in the ocean, or canoed on a quiet lake. Spending time in the outdoors has been critically important to me and to my well-being. Feeling the sun in my face, breathing fresh air, or feeling the flow of water over me have all made me feel close to God. Many have described a similar feeling. I recently reread *The Outermost House* by Henry Beston. He lived for a year in a small shack on the dunes of Cape Cod, less than fifty miles from where I grew up. In 1928, he wrote, "The world today is sick to its thin blood for lack of elemental things, for fire before the hands, for water welling from the earth, for air, for the dear earth itself underfoot."[7] Despite his austere environment, he goes on to describe the wondrous year he spent by the sea. While he does not profess any religion, he clearly felt a spiritual renewal by being close to nature. I think many of us would love to have such an experience. *~End~*

If one believes in a God who created the world, it is logical to assume that everything was created with a purpose. As the Psalmist says, "The heavens declare the glory of God; the skies proclaim the work of his hands."[8] The apostle Paul discusses this idea at the start of his letter to the church in Rome, "For since the creation of the world God's invisible qualities—His eternal power and divine nature—have been clearly seen, being understood from what has been made, so that men are without excuse."[9] In other words, the world around us was created in a way that would teach us, so our ability to discern the interconnected nature of our surroundings shows the importance of interconnections. If God created these interconnections, then it follows that God is communicating their importance.

Bryan: I have often observed something in nature and felt that God was communicating to me through what I saw. As a beekeeper, I am always amazed at how bees organize themselves and accomplish relatively enormous tasks. While each bee can only carry a fraction of an ounce of nectar from a flower back to the hive, the entire colony of bees can produce up to one hundred pounds of honey in a few weeks from the countless drops of nectar brought in. The bees do this work by flying miles away from the hive and finding their way back so as to get nectar from many sources. Other bees work inside the hive to dehydrate the nectar and cap the honey in comb cells. Somehow, the bees are communicating to do all this work. They appear to be in perfect harmony. Yet scientists have little idea how a bee communicates or navigates, as it is an insect with very little for a brain. My feeling is that God is using bees to show us the importance of social interconnections toward accomplishing goals for the common good. *~End~*

How should we interconnect? Humans are social creatures. The most popular websites today are social networks. Yet we find that many social connections are not only unsatisfying, but often destructive. The cyber-bullying of a social outcast. The dysfunctional marriage of a couple. The victimization of an individual by a crime. They all are negative connections. What is their common thread? How can we eliminate this destructiveness?

A social connection is defined as the mixing of people, and it can have good or bad outcomes. Truly positive social connections require that each person take a charitable interest in others. Each must overcome his or her selfish tendencies and instead focus on common priorities. Successfully married couples understand this concept. Marriage is a compromise of one's selfish interests for the sake of the marriage and the family. This type of social connection is satisfying and productive. But is there a more fundamental process at work? The strongest social connections are spiritual. They foster a bond between people and with God; they are based on compassion and empathy.

Bryan: As a teacher, I try to connect with my students from the start of the school year. I learned early on that this was a crucial first step in order to be an effective teacher. I don't always succeed, but when I do, the results are dramatic. For one thing, I have had consistently well behaved classes where the students get to work. For another, I have had many students with whom I have developed an appropriate, but close relationship, and who went on to achieve brilliant success. These positive outcomes did not happen because I was so good at presenting the material or managing the classroom. Instead, they happened because the students trusted me, and knew I cared about them, so they poured all their effort into learning. Many of them have stayed in contact with me. Such connections are far more valuable to me than any teaching award or salary increase. I think any teacher reading this would agree. *~End~*

Two

From Adam to Jesus

Background on Christian Thought

Humankind has mental, physical, social, and spiritual dimensions. From the beginning of known history, we have felt a spiritual connection with God, nature, and one another. Each culture has developed its spiritual view differently, but there are many commonalities. Faith in God is basically a spiritual connection with an omnipresent being who is benignly connected to all consciousness for eternity. Some people find this idea foolish and incomprehensible. Others are inspired to connect with God, sometimes against great opposition, and for reasons unclear to us. Yet all major faiths espouse the same notion: spiritual connections with people and with God are the most important and fulfilling goals of one's life.

The Judeo-Christian view is that God created humankind to be an independently thinking creature with a free will and with an innate spiritual connection to God. The story of Adam and Eve in the Garden of Eden tells us that they walked and talked with God. [10] However, the Bible then explains that humankind rebelled against God, so God banished humans to a life of hardship and toil. [11] Worse, the spiritual connection between God and humans was severed, as God can only be spiritually connected with those who seek Him, are harmonious with Him, and obedient to Him. The Bible defines the new disconnected condition of humankind as *sin*.[12] From that point forward, all humankind has been sinful, and it is up to each individual to personally find God. Christians believe we must first acknowledge our need for God and His love for us, demonstrated by His Son's sacrifice on our behalf, in order for us to be one with God.

Therefore, sometime in our ancient past, humankind entered a spiritual void where humans suddenly found themselves outside of God's presence. This spiritual void was the source of much evil in the world. As Paul explains:

> For although they knew God, they neither glorified him as God nor gave thanks to him, but their thinking became futile and their foolish hearts were darkened.

Although they claimed to be wise, they became fools and exchanged the glory of the immortal God for images made to look like mortal man and birds and animals and reptiles. Furthermore, since they did not think it worthwhile to retain the knowledge of God, he gave them over to a depraved mind, to do what ought not to be done.[13]

Humankind committed evil acts and self-centered worship in place of devoting itself to God and following His laws. Many struggled to regain the spiritual connection that had been lost. Early in the Bible, we see that Adam's grandson, Enosh is born and that "at that time, men began to call on the name of the Lord."[14] From that point, the Bible begins to introduce people who periodically connect with God and begin to reveal a true understanding of God to humankind. Christ presented the ultimate revelation.

An important point in the Christian view of spirituality is that while God has professed His unconditional love, each person must undergo an act of contrition before connecting with Him. God does not force Himself upon us, and He does not reject anyone. However, He discriminates in the way in which He connects, requiring us to acknowledge our need for Him. He also mandates that we form relationships with one another. Our modern society thwarts spiritual connections by interfering in how people connect with God and with one another. Our humanistic and materialistic official policies deny God. Our information-based economy thrives on change and fluid employment, destabilizing our personal lives and breaking up interpersonal relationships. The social flaws evident in our world today can be attributed to this interference.

The Bible gives guidance on how to connect spiritually with God and with one another, namely by loving God and loving one another. From the Old Testament, we have, "You shall love your neighbor as yourself."[15] Later on, Moses advises the Hebrew nation, "You shall love the Lord your God with all your heart, with all your soul, and with all your strength."[16] The word *love* in these passages is from the Hebrew word, *awhab*, meaning basic affection. [17] However, in the New Testament, Jesus quotes these passages to show that they are the key to spiritual connections:

> And behold, a certain lawyer stood up and tested Him [Jesus], saying, "Teacher, what shall I do to inherit eternal life?" He said to him, "What is written in the law? What is your reading of it?" So he answered and said, "You shall love the Lord your God with all your heart, with all your soul, with all your strength and with all your mind, and your neighbor as yourself." And He said to him, "You have answered rightly; do this and you will live."[18]

Eternal life really means an eternal connection with God, or a spiritual life. The word *love* here is from the Greek, *agape*, meaning social or moral love.[19] The King James Bible used to use the word *charity* to translate *agape*. A modern rendition would be *compassion*. In other words, it is not love in the romantic sense, but in a charitable, moral, and empathetic sense. Yet Jesus knew that this lawyer and every other person on earth were incapable of sustaining this position consistently through their own actions. What was needed was a connection with God that would enable them to begin to love in a godly way and to build and strengthen the spiritual connection they had with God and with others. Jesus came to earth to reconcile humankind with God and to enable this spiritual connection for all people. He made possible the correlation between a moral compass and a relationship with God, which is recognized by most ancient civilizations.

We needed this reconciliation, as God had broken off His connection with humankind when we rebelled against Him. Violence ensued upon the earth to the point that God had to wipe out all life with a great flood, except for Noah, his family, and some animals. Noah's descendants generally failed to connect with God, except for a few righteous people. God eventually chose a man, Abram, later known as Abraham, to father a race of chosen people, the Israelites. They were the descendants of Abraham's grandson, Jacob, or Israel. God gave this chosen people specific instructions on how they could connect with Him. God allowed a select few, the priests, to enter into His presence inside a tabernacle (a specially prepared tent and later a temple), designated by God as a holy place. There, the priests could intervene on behalf of the people through special rituals handed down by God.

Then, according to the Bible, God sent His son, Jesus Christ, to save all humankind, "For God so loved the world that He gave His only begotten Son that whoever believes in Him should not perish but have everlasting life."[20] Believing in Jesus goes farther than simply acknowledging His existence. It means believing in the saving power of His sacrifice on the cross. For in this act, Jesus took our sins onto Himself, suffered in our place to atone for these sins, and reconciled us with God. In other words, the fundamental tenet of Christian doctrine states that we must first believe in God and acknowledge our need for Him, then accept His gift to us: our salvation from sin through the sacrifice of his son, Jesus Christ.

Jesus explains this situation through various analogies and stories. He says to his disciples,

> I am the vine, and my Father is the vinedresser. Every branch in me that does not bear fruit He takes away; and every branch that bears fruit He prunes, that it may bear more fruit...Abide in Me, and I in you. As the branch cannot bear fruit of itself, unless it abides in the vine, neither can you, unless you abide in Me.[21]

One cannot effectively spread the word of God without first establishing his or her own connection with God through

Jesus. Living branches that bear fruit have the sap of the vine flowing into them, as fruitful believers have the spirit of God flowing into them.

Bryan: I became a Christian when I was around ten years old while listening to a Billy Graham crusade on television. I cannot explain why, but as I listened to Graham say that I only had to acknowledge my need for God and for Jesus, I prayed for God to accept me then and there. I had no prior religious upbringing, and I wasn't even in the same room as the television. It was down the hall! However, from that point on, I began to build a relationship with God, and I believe today that God's spirit has helped me and guided me through good and bad times. I have also felt the power of prayer when others have prayed for me. It is difficult to describe, but I would say it is a sense of serenity that most indicates God's spiritual presence. *~End~*

What is God's will? To love God and those around us. Jesus makes it clear that to love God means to follow His direction in life and ignore our own desires. Jesus says, "If you keep My commandments, you will abide in My love, just as I have kept My Father's commandments and abide in His love."[22] Essentially, to love God is to obey God. A spiritual connection with God requires us to obey His commandments. God's commandments represent the ultimate truth, the absolute standard of right and wrong. We are to uphold this standard, not debase it or modify it to our own liking. Yet, many problems today stem from a relativistic view of right and wrong, leading to moral chaos in which there is no standard of behavior.

God understands that we will continually fall short in our attempt to obey His commandments. Nobody is perfect. We must also not be legalistic with one another. Instead, we should pray for the strength to do what is right and to have compassion. We should ask for forgiveness when we fail. When we have a real relationship with God, then we will naturally want to do what is right. We are not just following a set of rules, but living in a new way. As David says in Psalm 19, "The law of the Lord is perfect, reviving the soul."[23]

Parents can see an analogous situation in the relationship with their children. When children obey, parents feel more connected to them than when the children rebel. Some families break up as teenage children become overly rebellious and disobedient, trying to live by a different standard than their parents. The biblical story of the prodigal son highlights this situation, and Jesus shows how God, the father in the story, is always ready to accept us back and connect with us after we recognize our disobedience and seek reconciliation with Him.[24] Yet many laws and rules in today's society encourage children to rebel against their parents, thereby fracturing this connection between parent and child.

One example is the passage of laws allowing minors to purchase contraception without parental consent. In our home state of Connecticut, children under sixteen years old can even get an abortion without parental consent. [25] Such laws are humanistic, focusing on "helping" the individual, while ignoring the effects on families and the community. This type of law abrogates the parents' authority to determine their child's behavior by allowing the child to bypass his or her parents with approval and protection from the state. As a result, parents feel compelled to watch and mistrust their children, and children feel compelled to sneak things past their parents. The end result is a deteriorated parent-child relationship.

If we consider that God has set up the parent-child relationship to teach us, then it makes sense that children will learn about obeying a higher authority by obeying their parents first. God makes it clear that children should obey their parents. "Honor your mother and father"[26] is number five of the Ten Commandments. At a young age, children do not understand the idea of God or His commandments, but they understand the relationship with their parents. Most children go through a rebellious phase as they begin to walk and talk, the so-called "terrible twos." If they learn that this rebelliousness is acceptable because their parents fail to discipline them, then how can they later learn to obey God? Learning to love and obey God is vital to connect with God spiritually.

"Love thy neighbor as thyself"[27] is the other requirement for a spiritual life. Jesus lived a life of charitable acts and kindness toward the most afflicted and outcast people, including lepers, prostitutes, and tax collectors. The same lawyer who had asked Jesus about eternal life also asked him, "And who is my neighbor?"[28] Jesus answered by telling the story of the good Samaritan.[29] A Samaritan was a religious outcast in Jewish eyes, as many people from Samaria comprised the lost tribes of Israel, displaced from the land and from the Jewish tradition. But Jesus showed how this Samaritan performed an outstanding act of charity for the victim of a highway robbery while some Jewish leaders walked quickly past and failed to get involved. Thus, the Samaritan was the neighborly one, as exemplified by his actions.

We should do likewise, so that in loving our neighbor, we reach out to whoever needs us, not just to those who appeal to us. This type of action is the *agape,* or spiritual love that God commands. Often, today's society prevents people from helping their neighbors due to concerns with liability and mistrust. A 2013 Associated Press poll found that less than one-third of Americans trust other people in their everyday lives, compared to about half in 1972.[30] Many people are charitable with their time and money, but these types of activities are different from directly helping a person in need, and thus do not yield the same type of connection.

Bryan: I had a strange occurrence happen to me when living in England many years ago. I was driving back to our village with my family on a cold, rainy winter day. All of a sudden, we saw an old woman walking down a remote section of a country road with a shopping cart. We passed by her, and my wife and I felt something was wrong. I dropped off my family at home and drove back to check on the woman. When I found her and stopped, I realized immediately that she was homeless. She was covered in mud and was shivering, pushing a beat up cart filled with ragged possessions. I asked her if I could help her, and she accepted a ride, so I loaded her and her gear into my car. I tried to get her to tell me where to go, thinking she might know of a shelter nearby, but she was like a child and could not give coherent directions. I stopped at a police station and a church, but neither could help me.

Finally, after hours of driving around, I called my wife. We both agreed to take in the woman for the night. Now we were a bit wary, but our home had an attached apartment, unconnected to our living area, so we put her up in there. My wife helped her clean up, then had her join us for dinner. The next day, I finally found a social worker who helped me move the woman into a temporary shelter. The whole incident was a unique experience for me. While I consider myself charitable, helping this woman and having her in my home was far outside my comfort zone. However, I felt that as soon as I began helping her, God was helping me. I felt His guidance throughout, and I felt His gratitude. I also felt a stronger connection to God than ever before. *~End~*

A key point in Christian belief is that a person must form spiritual connections with other people in order to spiritually connect with God. We cannot hate our neighbor and expect God to have a relationship with us. Jesus makes this clear in many parts of the Bible. From the Sermon on the Mount, He says, "Blessed are the merciful, for they shall obtain mercy." [31] A person who is merciful to another person can expect God to show mercy on him or her. Further on, He advises, "Therefore if you bring your gift to the altar, and there remember that your brother has something against you, leave your gift there before the altar and go your way. First be reconciled to your brother, and then come and offer your gift." [32] This indicates that one must have good interpersonal relations to form a good relationship with God. Paul sums up this case in his first letter to the church at Corinth, "And now abide faith, hope, love, these three; but the greatest of these is love." [33] The love he speaks of is *agape* or charity, and it is the most important quality for spiritual connection.

Bryan: Reconciling by saying sorry to someone can be tough. Yet I have found that the more I do it, the easier it gets. I have a tendency to put my foot in my mouth around people sometimes, and I end up offending them. I apologize frequently!

Nevertheless, I always find that I end up in an even better relationship with the person to whom I apologized, as he or she recognizes that I did not mean any harm and that I truly care about him or her. Such reconciliation is crucial to human interactions. Our competitive modern world often puts down apologizing as something "weak," but I say it requires real strength to show compassion when you may get hostility in return. Do it anyway, and feel the result: a strengthened spiritual connection with the other person and with God. *~End~*

This idea of love affected how Christian peoples reordered their communities. Beginning in early Christian times, people became far more charitable with one another. The Book of Acts describes early Christian communities helping and sharing with one another by pooling their resources, "Now the multitude of those who believed were of one heart and one soul; neither did anyone say that any of the things he possessed was his own but they had all things in common."[34] This charity was encouraged by the early church. And it was carried out in a society dominated by the pagan Roman empire, which imposed ruinous taxes on the population.

On the other hand, in the story of the rich man and the beggar, Lazarus, Jesus illustrates what the consequences are for one who does not seek spiritual connection through mercy, charity, and love. Lazarus the beggar sits outside the gate of a rich man in utter misery, but the rich man ignores him. Both men die. While Lazarus is taken up to heaven to be in the company of Abraham, the rich man is taken down to Hell. The rich man begs Abraham to let Lazarus relieve him, but Abraham says, "between us and you there is a great gulf fixed, so that those who want to pass from here to you cannot, nor can those from there pass to us."[35] Thus, by failing to form a spiritual connection between himself and Lazarus in life, the rich man condemned himself to a permanent disconnection from God and from others in death.

Finally, establishing spiritual connections with others and with God gives us a sense of peace and well-being that cannot come from any actions taken individually. We need connections with others to thrive and survive. We need a connection with God to receive His strength and support as we face worldly challenges. As Paul explains to the early church at Phillipi:

> Be anxious for nothing, but in everything by prayer and supplication, with thanksgiving, let your requests be made known to God; and the peace of God, which surpasses all understanding, will guard your hearts and minds through Christ Jesus.[36]

Three

Seeking Harmony

Background on Other Spiritual Beliefs

Despite significant differences, all faiths possess basic commonalities. The belief that humankind has a spiritual aspect involving God and others is common in all religions. The central tenet of Islam, Zen Buddhism, and Native American beliefs is that humankind exists in a spiritually interconnected world, and that achieving harmony with God (or universal spirituality) and all other life should be our ultimate aim. These three faiths have unanimously condemned the modern world for its lack of spirituality and its disconnected nature. We focused on these three because Bryan has some personal experience with them. They also serve as excellent examples of faiths that appear to be very different, yet show the common traits that highlight the premise of this book.

In the editor's introduction (1979) of the book, *Toward Understanding Islam*, Khurshid Ahmad explains that *Islam* is derived from two words, *salm*, which means *peace*, and *silm*, which means *submission*. The entire meaning of the word *Islam* is "a commitment to surrender one's will to the Will of God."[37] He goes on to explain:

> Harmonization of man's will with the Will of God leads to the harmonization of different spheres of life under an all-embracing ideal. Departmentalization of life into different water-tight compartments, religious and secular, sacred and profane, spiritual and material, is ruled out. There is unity of life and unity of the source of guidance...Each and every act becomes related to God and his guidance. Every human activity is given a transcendent dimension; it becomes sacred and meaningful and goal-centred.[38]

Harmony and unity both imply some form of a connection. Islam believes that all humans are born in a naturally connected state with God, but some drift away from this ideal condition. Later in the book, the author, Abul A'la Mawdudi, writes, "The man who denies God is called *Kafir* (concealer) because he conceals *by his disbelief* what is inherent in his nature and embalmed in his soul."[39] He goes on to describe the disbeliever as a witness of all of God's creation who cannot comprehend that God is behind it. This type of person will find that "his entire existence will be unsatisfactory...and his evil activities will make life bitter for him and for all around him."[40] Disconnectedness from God results in evil behavior and is caused by ignoring the spiritual realm all around us. Yet how often is this spiritual realm discussed or pondered in our lives today? Very little for many people. Is it any wonder then that we see the increase in discontent and evil in our modern society?

In contrast, the person who believes in God has a sustaining faith and trust in Him. This person also naturally acts charitably toward others. Mawdudi explains, "This faith imparts to his heart extraordinary consolation, fills it with satisfaction and keeps it filled with hope."[41] Muslims believe that Islam is the natural faith of all humankind who have seen the Creation and believe in God as the Creator, even of those who lived before the time of the Prophet Mohammad.[42] As in the Christian faith, compassion for one's fellow humans is integral to the spiritual connection one has with God.

Zen Buddhism is a branch of Mahayana Buddhism, primarily found in Japan. Zen is not a religion in the Western sense, but more of a way of life, a life that must be experienced to be understood. The Japanese word for Buddhism is *shu do*, meaning *middle way*, or a way of life that is spiritually centered and balanced. In *Questions to a Zen Master*, the master explains that the middle way does not imply compromise or indecision. Instead, it is a synthesis of the spiritual and material:

> The chief characteristic of European civilization is dualism. Materialism, for example, is opposed to

spiritualism...but in reality the material and spiritual are one and cannot stand in opposition to each other...Spiritual is material and material becomes spiritual. Mind exists in every one of our cells and ultimately mind itself is body and the body itself is mind...*The middle way integrates everything.*[43]

This passage expresses a view of the interconnectedness of spirituality. He goes on to say, "Our life is connected to the cosmic power and stands in a relation of interdependence with all other existences. We cannot live by ourselves...so we must not become selfish."[44] He also explains, "So where does the ego [our individuality] exist? It is one with the cosmos. It is not only the body, the mind, but it is God, Buddha, the fundamental cosmic force."[45] We are one with God, and with all others, completely connected. Zen is an attempt to discard the worldly distractions around us and to perceive this interconnectedness through meditation, or *zazen*. The master eloquently reiterates this idea:

> People who are ambitious and full of desire are always searching for freedom but they can't find it. They are always worried and sad, their desires keep growing and growing, and in the end they fall ill or become neurotic. *Freedom does not mean doing whatever you like.* Too much gratification of desires does not lead to freedom because human desires are limitless...To remain peaceful always, and not anxious, is best. And in that way, through *zazen*, we can regulate desires as they arise.[46]

In other words, through meditation and a sense of oneness with God and all existence, one is able to find peace and discard superfluous desires. This is a return to the natural state we are in at birth, connected to the eternal consciousness. The author continues, "The ultimate dimension, in the very depths of being, the supreme dimension of life, is universal consciousness and love."[47] As in Judeo-Christian thought, Zen teaches that the ultimate way is one of love and compassion toward others. The master states that a Zen believer must first bring tranquility to himself or herself through *zazen*, before being able to commune in harmony with others.

Native American beliefs vary by tribe, but there are two common, basic beliefs. In *Native American Religion in Early America*, Christine Leigh Heyrman describes these as the belief in an "all-powerful, all-knowing Creator or 'Master Spirit,'" and the belief in the afterlife, or immortality, which is a period of happiness and plenty.[48] Native Americans also believe that all living creatures have spirits, and therefore that all life has to be respected. Heyrman summarizes this idea:

> The most important [concept] is that Indians did not distinguish between the natural and the supernatural. On the contrary, Native Americans perceived the "material" and "spiritual" as a unified realm of being—a kind of extended kinship network. In their view, plants, animals and humans partook of divinity through their close connection with "guardian spirits," a myriad of

"supernatural" entities who imbued their "natural" kin with life and power.[49]

Again, we see the key idea of spiritual interconnection between the Creator and the creation. Native Americans did not consider spirituality a separate realm. The world they lived in was both spiritual and material.

In all these faiths, Islam, Zen Buddhism, Native American religion, and the Judeo-Christian, we see the same basic idea of a spiritual connection. All express belief in a Creator God who is linked to humankind when we are in harmony with Him, with one another, and with the created world in which we live. Similarly, being in disharmony with God results in a disconnected state of unhappiness and even evil.

To disregard the central message in all these faiths is pure arrogance, as it assumes we are wiser than the countless generations of faithful people who came before us. However, that is exactly the predominant social attitude in our mainstream media and public institutions. Our society tolerates the existence of faith, but treats it as a sideshow, generally inappropriate or unworthy of consideration in public discourse. Spirituality is barred from serious consideration when it comes to news coverage, public policy, or public education. Therefore, each of us must work on our own to bring back a spiritual sense to our lives. Otherwise, we face a miserable existence as partial human beings, denying our most important attribute, our spirituality.

Four

The Good Old Days...Maybe Not

Spiritual Connections in Traditional Society

It would be inaccurate to say that today's society is completely devoid of spirituality compared to the past. Since the birth of sin, human society has had problems. It is more helpful to examine how people formed spiritual connections in the past, how these may have been affected by modern developments, and how we can use that knowledge to form spiritual connections today. Traditional society, especially before the Industrial Revolution, had a stability that enabled spiritual connections without the constant disruption of change, our great bane today.

Historically, the traditional family, often encompassing extended networks of people, played a huge role in forming spiritual connections. Before modern social programs were enacted, the family was both the insurance agent and the welfare agent for a family member in need. As this sense of reliance has diminished, relationships have suffered as well. Additionally, sons often worked for their fathers, so the family was the employer and provider to many people. Ancestor worship was also a major component of familial ties. Even today, many Asian families have a shrine in their home dedicated to their ancestors. These people gain strength from the spiritual connection with their forebears.

Probably the most intense spiritual connection within a family is between a mother and her child, as it begins in the womb. There are countless anecdotes of a mother who correctly sensed something had happened to her child, even though the mother and child were separated and could not communicate. While writing this book, I saw *Rabbit-Proof Fence*, a movie about three mixed-race Australian girls who escape from a government detention center so that they can go home to their mothers. The Australian government, up until 1970, believed that mixed-race children, all of whom were born out of wedlock from white fathers and aboriginal mothers, were better off away from their aboriginal homes and were put in a government-run center. This policy ignored the spiritual connection between mothers and children, and it ignored the detrimental effect of separating them. At the end of the movie, the girls are reunited with their mothers, and it is evident that the true power of the spiritual connection between mother and daughter is what motivated each girl to keep going. Such a strong connection can only be explained in spiritual terms.

Of course, a family may be dysfunctional and cruel to its members, so traditional families were not necessarily better in the past. Many people have stories of a family member who ran away to escape a bad family situation. What has changed is that people today in most developed countries do not feel as strong a tie to their families as they once did, because they do not have to rely on their families as much. However, they are also more likely to start a family for reasons relating to love and affection, rather than as a survival tactic. The family remains one of the most important social institutions by which a person can connect spiritually with others.

Another key social institution in all cultures was the village, an entity that ingrained the concept of community and group effort into the minds of its inhabitants. The village offered stability in two ways: stability in people and stability in location. Families would live in a village for generations. As one grew up, he or she would know the same people during his or her entire lifetime. Moreover, the village stayed where it was and rarely moved. The people knew the land around them intimately.

Many cultures felt strong ties to the land and would fight for their right to live on it. A dramatic example was in England in the 1600s when the Earl of Bedford led an effort to drain the fens, the vast marshland in eastern England. [50] By most standards, this was an improvement of the land, as the fens were portrayed as trackless marshes with little economic output and much disease. Yet, the fen natives fought the change violently, persistently sabotaging the draining efforts. The fen people felt an attachment to the marshes. As inhospitable as the marshes may have seemed to others, the fen people fought to keep them unchanged. In the end, they lost. Today, the fens are some of the richest farmland in England, though they are very thinly populated.

Another aspect of village life was that many things were done in a communal way, so that everyone felt connected and committed to the community's well-being. Examples include the Amish community's practice of raising a barn, the traditional Asian community's practice of planting and harvesting rice, and the Inuit community's practice of hunting together. All of these activities involved mutual aid and survival, so participation was crucial. Such activities forged considerable bonds of trust among the participants. Similarly, villagers participated in communal festivals, which were often religious in nature. Christian villages celebrated various feast days throughout the year, and as a person grew up, these festivals not only marked the time of year, but also gave a sense of timelessness, as traditions were kept.

Bryan: I grew up in a small New England village and felt close to the community. As a boy, I knew almost every resident on my street and the main streets in town. I used to sell tickets to Boy Scout dinners by going door to door, and I was often invited in for a minute. I was between eleven and fourteen years old, and I was doing this alone. It never occurred to me or my parents that any of these people would harm me in any way, and none of them ever did. Yet today, who among us as parents would allow our children to go door to door unescorted? Sadly, we generally do not trust our neighbors anymore.

However, I do not believe people have become more evil. Instead, I think we have lost the connections with our neighbors, so they have become unknown to us. Our neighborhoods are no longer communal. Working to change our neighborhoods to restore these connections and a sense of trust would do much to help people feel reconnected to their fellow human beings. Some neighborhoods and communities have attempted to reconnect people through social events, such as neighborhood block parties, community festivals, and other special events. Nevertheless, the most effective way to build connections is for each person to make an effort to know his or her neighbors and to help anyone in need. Acts of charity and compassion that

35

come from the heart will forge strong spiritual connections.
~End~

It is important to note that village life was not necessarily ideal. Villagers have been notoriously suspicious of outsiders and intolerant of anyone different from their idea of the norm. Also, while it can be very nice to celebrate the same festivals year after year, it also requires a special mind-set to seek God and maintain a true relationship with God if one repeats the same ceremony of worship in a religious festival time after time. The Protestant Reformation, and especially Puritanism, led to a rejection of old religious traditions and the cancellation of the old festivals, as the Protestant leaders felt they had become mindless exercises or even ungodly celebrations. These festivals encouraged a connection within the village, but not necessarily with other communities or with God.

Finally, people often felt security and stability in their work, and this generated good interpersonal connections in the workplace. Until a century ago, the majority of people worked on a farm.[51] A farmer would try to have a large family, ensuring plenty of help around the farm. His children often joined him and worked the farm, until eventually inheriting it. Sometimes, they ran away to escape the drudgery of farm life. Farmers often had hired hands who worked and lived with the family. Sometimes, these people became part of the family, though sometimes they remained outside it.

Today, this farming life seems idyllic, but in reality it was a very tough existence. In *Post-Capitalist Society*, his review of economic history leading up to today's changing world, Peter Drucker points out that when the Industrial Revolution came along with its steady factory jobs, many agricultural workers "flocked to the factory precisely because they were still better off there than they were at the bottom of a static, tyrannical, and starving rural society."[52] While this migration of people from farms and villages to factory towns and cities was based on economic improvement, it also separated people from one another and enfeebled their spiritual connections.

Nowadays, many people face a similar choice: either stay where they live in poverty, but among friends and family, or move to a new place that promises prosperity, but far from everyone they know and love. It is not an easy choice. Each person must weigh the benefits and costs of both options. Our only advice is to properly value the spiritual connections that one has so that the final decision accounts for all costs, not just the material ones. Many people have learned the hard way that a supposedly promising move to a richer life has ended up being a lonely venture where the material gain was not worth the spiritual connections that were lost.

Although a traditional society may not necessarily make people connect spiritually, it encourages the idea of mutual trust. In trusting one another, people are more likely to form relationships, which facilitate a more spiritual life. We could learn from this example by instilling trust in others and working to form strong social bonds with our peers. However, strong families, villages, and farms were only as spiritually alive as their members. It is tempting to think that these people held a strong sense of spirituality that we are missing, but they also had to struggle at times to make spiritual connections. What they had in their favor was a sense of stability in their lives that allowed them to form spiritual connections at a natural pace. For us today, as the world around us changes ever more rapidly, we feel forced to live accordingly. Nevertheless, we still need to seek God, ask for His help, and establish the vital spiritual connections we need to live.

Five

Life at the Speed of Light

The Information Society's Destructive Effects

The *information society* is the economic age in which we find ourselves. In an anthology on this subject, Frank Webster, professor of sociology, explains:

> There is within current social science a view, frequently advanced, that information is now more central to our way of life, so much so that many scholars conceive of the emergence of a new entity, the Information Society. From this perspective the Information Society is seen to be as different from Industrialism as the Industrial Society was from its predecessor, the Agricultural Society...in the Information Society livelihoods are increasingly made by the appliance and manipulation of

information...and the output is not so much a tangible
thing as a change in image, relationship or perception.[53]

The key idea here is that we are in a new economic age, and the main economic product of the information society is change itself. In other words, stability in our lives is decreasing. Whatever we find around us today is likely to change or be gone tomorrow. Information is the new commodity, and it can move at the speed of light. How should we react to this? It is up to each person to face these changes in his or her own way. However, from a spiritual point of view, we are challenged to form a perpetual connection with God while living in an ever-changing world. Our relationships with each other will also be more difficult to maintain, as the people around us are more susceptible to change.

One change we see in the information society is the increasing rate of alterations in the workplace. In "Is Britain the First Post-Industrial Society?" John Urry states, "Modern society is the first known society in which the dominant class has a vested interest in change, transformation, and in dissolving economic and social relations as fast as they can be established."[54] He explains that in the transformation to a post-industrial society, the economic forces for progress have accelerated the pace of change to continuously accommodate the changes in the market. However, these changes also destabilized the social order. He notes that in Britain this rapid change has caused a reactionary nostalgia for the industrial past, as it represented a seemingly more stable society than that of today.[55]

Bryan: I have seen immense changes in the workplace in my lifetime. Many people commute farther and farther to gain a better position, and all of us work longer hours than ever before. Yet it is difficult to explain why we do this. Upon reflection, it appears somewhat illogical, as the changes rarely bring more happiness, but they always add more stress. My wife and I have talked about simplifying our lives. I think many other people have reached the same conclusion. Today's workplace is ever more ruthless and competitive, but promises fewer and fewer rewards for the competitor. It also is harder and harder to socially connect at work, as people come and go more frequently, and competition gets ever more keen. We should all examine our position and reflect on how we can achieve a spiritually healthy career. Perhaps our income will drop, but if our social connections and overall spiritual well-being improve, we should consider that worth the lost income. *~End~*

Manuel Castells explains the effect of this accelerated pace of change in "An Introduction to the Information Age" by stating, "There is a tremendous anxiety and discontent about work." [56] He goes on to describe how the information age economy, based on the global networking of labor and capital, is leading to a situation where most work will be done by temporary, part-time, contract employees, rather than long-term, full-time, traditional employees. He goes on to say, "As a result of these trends, most societies in the world...with the US and UK at the top of the scale, present powerful trends towards increasing inequality, social polarization and social exclusion."[57] He expounds that the global economy has funneled wealth to fewer people, leaving the majority economically insecure or impoverished. He wrote this book sixteen years ago. The trend has only gotten worse, as the United States has suffered an economic crisis since 2008 that has sidelined millions of people from stable employment, while the major banks that triggered the crisis have all recovered and prospered. Despite one's view of the economic situation, it is clear that it has generated divisions in society and a feeling of insecurity and general distrust.

The change in the workplace precipitates changes in families and communities as well. Peter Drucker explains that "organizations in the post-capitalistic society thus constantly upset, disorganize, and destabilize the community." [58] He discusses how the changes wrought by the information society have disintegrated traditional organizations. He concludes that people still need mutual support, so they need to build a community from whoever happens to be around. He offers no concrete recommendations, and he never mentions spirituality.

A second change in the information society, driven by this need for community, is the advent of *social networking,* or the electronically enabled linking up of humans all over the globe. The world is often described as "interconnected" or a "global community." While the Internet and all its available services allow people to communicate electronically all around the globe, the vast majority of these communications are impersonal and unspiritual. Much of the traffic on the Internet is merely driven by commerce. E-mail accounts are constantly deluged with commercial solicitations, and every website is polluted with advertisements and pop-up scams. However, the most common trend on the Internet is social networking, where people can post their latest thoughts, photos, or videos and allow others to see them and respond. Aside from interactions with existing friends or relatives, this type of communication tends to be shallow and unsatisfying. Lisa Haisha, founder of the Whispers From Children's Hearts Foundation, describes this trend in her blog:

> We're seeing an incredible retreat into virtual worlds these days. People are hiding behind their monitors more than ever before, and their time spent online continues to climb. What this means is less human interaction, less touch, less accountability, and less human connection. That can be a sure sign of loneliness. In fact, the use of social media sites, when gone unchecked, can actually exacerbate feelings of loneliness, because they remind the user of how little interaction they truly have with others.[59]

Many have found that social networking does the opposite of what it is promoted to do. It makes people feel isolated, not connected. Unlike real life with its ups and downs, the life portrayed on social networking sites tends to consist of only positive experiences. It is a very one-sided view of life. As a result, a person who is suffering from some negative experience will look at a social network and not see anyone else suffering. He or she will feel very alone, and the physical separation from fellow human beings will magnify this feeling of isolation.

Maggie: It's interesting that as our phones seem to become "smarter" and more savvy about what is going on around them, we consumers seem to suffer the reverse effect. The average person spends three or more hours a day social networking. We are so obsessed with the Internet that we frequently neglect our immediate environment. Engagement with a device in the presence of others subtly evokes the sense that the phone is more important, more interesting, and more worthwhile than the people present. I can't remember the last time I was at a restaurant and didn't see a nearby table with one or more people sacrificing conversation for the use of their phones. We are losing our sense of social graces and our sense of awareness regarding what is going on around us. Our phones are more cultured than we are. This behavior has become the "norm;" it is not at all taboo to interrupt a face-to-face conversation in order to send a text message. This behavior distances us from one another. It facilitates the deterioration of the spiritual connections we share with each other. *~End~*

Thus, despite all its hype, social networking is perhaps more anti-social than being alone. It is difficult to imagine developing a friendship with someone one has never met in person. On the contrary, one may become "friends" online with a person who is masquerading as someone he or she is not. This type of dishonesty can become quite sinister when an adult uses it to fool a child online into believing that he or she is another child. Moreover, the physical separation from one another can allow some people to act in a far more aggressive way via the Internet than they would in a face-to-face confrontation. People send highly inflammatory e-mails in situations where they may have kept their mouths shut in a personal encounter. Even worse, people online will quickly gather co-conspirators to harass or hurt someone with whom they have a disagreement. This problem has gotten so serious with teenagers that many states have passed legislation and rules on how to deal with this *cyberbullying*. All of this makes the modern social networking a personal minefield where people have to tread carefully so as not to set off a chain reaction of emotional explosions. This hardly lends itself to strong interpersonal and spiritual relationships.

A third change in the information society that actually hurts the formation of a community is the increasing division between those who are connected and those who are not. Pippa Norris refers to this situation as the *digital divide* and explains that it involves a "global divide" in "internet access between industrialized and developing nations," a "social divide...between information rich and poor in each nation," and a "democratic divide...between those who do, and do not, use the panoply of digital resources to engage, mobilize and participate in public life."[60] These divisions separate people in different ways, all of which hinder interpersonal and spiritual connections.

A fourth change in the information society that also hurts communities is the increased reality that we are under surveillance. Surveillance can take many forms. David Lyon describes four "strands" of surveillance theory: *nation state surveillance*, such as FBI or police surveillance; *bureaucratic surveillance*, such as government requirements to carry a driver's license and have a Social Security number; *technologic surveillance*, such as speed cameras and other high tech methods; and *political-economic surveillance*, such as how search engine companies track our Internet use to determine how we think as consumers. He shows that computers and the Internet have enabled all these types of surveillance to be increased dramatically.[61] Recent news reports have shown that the US National Security Agency secretly obtained Internet and telephone transaction records on US citizens, ostensibly to track down possible terrorists. Regardless of the government's motives, if we feel we are being monitored, we are less trusting and less willing to expose ourselves. This reluctance to communicate translates into weaker interpersonal connections.

So how do we negotiate these changes that are hurting our ability to connect spiritually? As in the face of all adversity, we seek God's help to face our challenge. In fact, all these changes present an opportunity for spiritual connections. Peter Drucker says that more charitable work is needed to help those who have been unemployed, dispossessed, or disconnected by all the changes in the information society.[62] He also says that there is a need to build new communities of people, but that "the community that is needed in post-capitalist society...has to be based on *commitment and compassion* rather than being imposed by proximity and isolation."[63] In other words, he is proposing that we connect with like-minded people wherever they are on the globe, instead of trying to connect with whoever happens to be around us. His proposal is problematic, for if we have a hard time now connecting with those around us, then it is logical it will be even harder to connect with those who are far away.

A more helpful proposal is to understand that the people around us will change, probably more frequently as time goes on, but that our mission is to connect with them, in person, however we can, for as long as they are around. Connecting with people far away using the Internet is nonsensical, as such a connection is inherently impersonal. Establishing a first-time connection can only be effective in person.

Bryan: During my twenty years in the United States Air Force, my family and I moved several times to new assignments, and the people at each duty station moved in and out while we were there. Nevertheless, the culture among military people was to make friends quickly with whoever was around and to help one another with any issues that came up. This was especially true overseas, as none of us had family nearby to rely on. We still stay in touch with many people who we met over the years. This type of shared commitment to form a community with whoever is around, despite the social turmoil of people's moving in and out, could serve as a model for today's society. *~End~*

Six

Me First

Secular Humanism's Destructive Effects

Many societal forces stymie the development of spiritual connections. In many countries, including the United States, the government is increasingly hostile toward any traditional religion. For those already spiritually connected to God, this only presents an inconvenience. As Paul says in his letter to the church at Rome, "For I am convinced that neither death, nor life, nor angels, nor heavenly rulers, nor things that are present, nor things to come, nor powers, nor height, nor depth, nor anything else in creation will be able to separate us from the love of God in Christ Jesus our Lord."[64] This implies that once the connection with God is established, it cannot be broken. However, for those unfamiliar with God, society's attacks on God can cause them to either be ignorant of Him or to question His validity in their lives.

In the United States, societal forces against God are politically driven by certain factions. They promote secularism, the removal of spirituality and religion from any public forum. The government caters to these factions, ostensibly to avoid any display of favoritism to one religion or another. Usually, the excuse given is "separation of church and state," an approximate citation of the First Amendment of the US Constitution. However, what this portion of the First Amendment actually says is, "Congress shall make no law respecting an establishment of religion, or prohibiting the free exercise thereof."[65] The reason for this amendment was to prevent the US government from establishing an official, state religion, a practice that was prevalent in Europe at the time of the Constitution's ratification.

However, interpretations of this amendment have stretched its meaning to prohibit not only Congress, but also state and local governments and any governmental institution from expressing religion in any way. This prohibition has led to the ridiculous extreme of people fearing to say, "Merry Christmas" in public or from having Christmas displays on town properties. In response, we have the equally ridiculous passing of a law in Texas legalizing the utterance of "Merry Christmas" in public places. Given these measures, it is hardly possible for people of any faith to express their beliefs openly without fear of recrimination.

We are not advocating for some sort of spiritual activism, such as prayer in schools or other measures called for by some religious factions. Instead, we are only describing the situation that exists when one person hopes to express his or her spiritual views to another. For a spiritual person who is truly connected to God, these prohibitions against religious expression are merely a speed bump, but for those unfamiliar with spirituality, they further their ignorance. Also, as some pro-religious groups have gotten politically active to fight the prohibition of religious expression, nonreligious bystanders see the fight as yet another unappealing display of political factions at work. As a result, an increasing number of people in the United States have no daily thought of God, nobody to talk to about God, and no real knowledge of God. This makes it difficult for those who feel spiritually connected to God to relate to people who do not believe in Him. Perhaps this is a challenge that God has put before them.

Much of this change in thinking toward spirituality and toward a belief in God has been due to the rise of humanism. The humanistic view existed in ancient times among some philosophers, but became resurgent during the end of the Middle Ages, with the start of the Renaissance, and later, in the Enlightenment. [66] These two terms, *Renaissance* and

Enlightenment, were invented by the intelligentsia who despised the medieval way of thinking. The Renaissance was a rebirth of a more disciplined, classical way of reasoning, and the Enlightenment went further by rejecting the biblical authority that had dominated Western thought for fifteen hundred years and had suppressed pagan and classical concepts. The framers of the US Constitution were products of the Enlightenment, though tempered by the Protestant beliefs that were prevalent in the American colonies. They believed in rational thought and scientific progress, and many had faith in a higher spiritual being.

Humanism seems positive in its intentions, but results in two negative consequences: the elevation of the individual's interests over the community's, and the rejection of any higher authority, especially of supernatural authority, which results in the denial of any higher moral code. Humanism is an intellectual philosophy; it is a product of thought, not of faith. As such, it comes from the mind of each individual and is defined by each individual. The Bible warns, "There is a way that seems right to a man, but in the end, it leads to death."[67] Therefore, as each person defines his or her own standards, there is bound to be conflict among people of different standards. In a spiritual union of people, everyone agrees on a universal standard of right and wrong, but in a humanistic society, no one agrees on any standard, as right and wrong become relative to each person's point of view. The ensuing conflict engulfs every aspect of society, as we are witnessing today. Nothing is agreed upon; everything is a source of contention.

Humanists see each person as a unique individual who should be guarded and nurtured in his or her lifetime—even to the detriment of the community. For example, the state, guided by humanist policies, houses and feeds prisoners, many guilty of violent crimes, then paroles them as early as possible. Humanists uphold these types of actions as just, as they believe that life on the earth is all there is, so they carefully try to protect it. Unfortunately, paroled criminals now have little fear of retribution and go on to commit more crimes. According to a study by the Connecticut Department of Correction, within five years of release, "79 percent [of parolees] were re-arrested, 69 percent were convicted of a new crime, and 50 percent were returned to prison with a new sentence."[68] Given these statistics, how can people trust one another, especially strangers? People are less likely to want to spiritually connect if they distrust or even fear those around them, and so communities break down.

Humanists believe that they can define good and evil on their own, without guidance from God. This change in thought caused chaotic political movements, such as the French Revolution. Intellectual leaders seized control by terrorizing the populace of France, making up laws as they went along, and defining good and evil as it suited them. Robespierre, the intellectual who led the Reign of Terror, which was the most murderous period of the French Revolution, rationalized the summary executions of tens of thousands of fellow French citizens using his own interpretation of justice.[69] Ironically, he later met the same fate under someone else's interpretation of justice.

The Communist revolutions would follow the same playbook, most notoriously in Cambodia under the Khmer Rouge. They slaughtered about two million people (one quarter of the country's population) who failed to meet the Khmer Rouge's criteria for "purity."[70] According to Youk Chhang of the *Cambodia Tribunal Monitor*, "A large proportion of the Cambodian people have mental problems because their family members were lost and their spirits damaged."[71] These radical political movements promoted faith in the state over faith in God, were often overtly atheistic, and were spiritually destructive.

Bryan: A simpler example of how humanism has changed society is in the way parents react to other people's children, especially their misbehavior. When I was a boy, any of my friend's parents felt perfectly justified in speaking to me if I misbehaved. They never disciplined me, but they would chastise me. Furthermore, if they reported my bad behavior to my parents, then my parents never questioned them, but dealt with me as if they had witnessed the bad behavior themselves. How

54

differently most parents act today. If a child misbehaves, I rarely see another parent intervene, and if it does happen, the child's parent usually becomes indignant. Today, different parents often have very different views of right and wrong, especially in regard to child behavior. Additionally, parents are much less trusting of others, and much more likely to suspect something evil. All of this dissension prevents a sense of communal responsibility for children and stunts spiritual connection among parents. *~End~*

In contrast to secularism and humanism, a traditional Judeo-Christian view of humankind believes each person is primarily spiritual and that our time on the earth is only a moment in eternity. The apostle Peter paraphrases the prophet Isaiah to make this point, "All flesh is as grass, and all the glory of man as the flower of the grass. The grass withers and its flower falls away, but the word of the Lord endures forever."[72] In comparison to the eternity of God, our human life is short and inconsequential. Therefore, during our time on earth, it is of the utmost importance to connect spiritually with God and with one another, as this is our only chance, as far as we know. What happens to us after death is not fully understood, but it is not something to be feared. Rather, it is only the end of our brief time on earth, and the start of our eternal, spiritual connection with God. Under this view, individuals must obey God and submit to the community, as the spiritual interconnection that makes up a community is key to helping each person build his or her connection with God.

Therefore, in this secular and humanist society in which we live, each of us must first examine his or her spiritual life, then find ways to improve it. Nobody will do this for us. As we establish or strengthen our relationship with God, we also should establish and strengthen relationships with those around us. As we do, we will begin to feel a common bond and sense of common purpose and common ethics. God's influence on us will ensure this change. Once we truly feel spiritually connected, then we will also feel a sense of harmony and true community spirit. We may spend a lifetime attempting to make all this happen, but the alternative is to live a stunted life as selfish individuals, robbed of any hope of spiritual peace.

Seven

Seeing Is Believing

Materialism's Destructive Effects

Perhaps the most fundamental antithesis to spirituality today is the culture of materialism, a concept that originated in Western society and has spread around the world through globalization. Materialism, like humanism, came about in modern times following the Renaissance. It denies any supernatural power or being and looks only to the material world to explain things. Materialism is the idea that reality is based solely on what we can interpret with our five senses. Spirituality and anything that cannot be scientifically proven using the standard scientific method is rejected as something superstitious or unreal.

Materialism was the intellectual answer to the mixture of religion, superstition, and frequently weak reasoning that had dominated Western philosophy and science through the Middle Ages. Beginning in the Renaissance, and especially during the Enlightenment, materialism became the primary philosophy of the scientific community. Materialism forced scientists to focus on the observable facts and to theorize using only these facts. The result has been an explosion of scientific discoveries and technological innovations for the past five hundred years. However, many of the original scientists who followed a materialistic approach in their labs still maintained a strong spiritual view of the world. Nevertheless, over time, materialism has gained supremacy in all public thought so that it has smothered spirituality in Western society and now, in much of the world.

In the view of each faith examined thus far, the idea of splitting the spiritual and material worlds is unreal and contrived. Reality is a seamless blend of the two worlds. In fact, people of both the Christian and Islamic faiths consider a disregard for the spiritual and an emphasis on the material to be a spiritual death sentence. Zen Buddhists and Native Americans find the idea of splitting the spiritual and material worlds nonsensical. In all cases, the spiritual dimension of life is vitally important, and a serious imbalance occurs when it is ignored.

While materialism as a philosophy is most prevalent in the scientific community, not all scientists have been purely materialistic. In fact, many renowned scientists have found that science and spirituality can be compatible. Fritjof Capra is one example we have already mentioned. Another is Francis S. Collins, M.D., Ph.D., currently the director of the National Institutes of Health. He also oversaw the mapping of the human genome. He is a globally acclaimed geneticist and an outspoken Christian. He believes in God and in the need for a spiritual life. Collins came to this conclusion as a young man, after growing up with an atheistic mind-set. Through his medical practice and experience with patients, Collins encountered people with faith. As he observed these patients, he began to question their notions. After some time, he spoke with a Methodist minister who introduced him to the writings of C.S. Lewis. As Collins describes, he came to believe in God as he looked on God's creation and read Lewis's treatise on faith and the idea of moral law. Collins explains:

> Lewis argues that if you are looking for evidence of a God who cares about us as individuals, where could you more likely look than within your own heart at this very simple concept of what's right and what's wrong. And there it is. Not only does it tell you something about the fact that there is a spiritual nature that is somehow written within our hearts, but it also tells you something about the nature of God himself, which is that he is a good and holy God. What we have there is a glimpse of what he stands for.[73]

The word *materialism* has also come to describe the personal seeking of pleasure through the acquisition of material goods. In this aspect, God is not only rejected, but completely neglected as a source of pleasure or happiness. One example is the corruption of Christmas, originally a celebration of the birth of God's Son, redeemer of all humankind, into a shopping frenzy that leaves the participants exhausted, depressed, and ill-tempered. The Bible warns against such materialism and points out its dangers. King Solomon recounts his pursuit of wealth and material pleasure, showing that it leaves him empty:

> Whatever my eyes desired I did not keep from them. I did not withhold my heart from any pleasure, for my heart rejoiced in all my labor; and this was my reward from all my labor. Then I looked on all the works that my hands had done and on the labor in which I had toiled; and indeed all was vanity and grasping for the wind. There was no profit under the sun.[74]

Pursuing material happiness is a fruitless exercise. This can include the pursuit of wealth, power, prestige, or pleasure. All of them lead to nothing, as Solomon found.

Bryan: I am saddened by how much our society has given itself over to material acquisition. At the time of this book's writing, several famous stores have announced they would open on Thanksgiving morning and begin the start of Christmas shopping even earlier than before. A few people have pointed out that the employees of these stores now face a day of work instead of a day of thanks, but most people accept the change. Two years ago, shoppers in Long Island actually trampled people in their stampede to get the best bargains during this notorious shopping period. This behavior is not only unspiritual and inhuman, it is insane.

A much better approach is to forget about shopping, spend time with friends and family, or volunteer to help others. When I was stationed in England ten years ago, my wife and I found the relatively slower paced lifestyle and lack of shopping mania so refreshing at the holidays. Since living there, we have slowed down and minimized holiday purchases. We enjoy our family time, and we reflect more on what we have. In the end, even a small change to reduce this materialistic approach to life can yield big benefits. *~End~*

Jesus warns against a materialistic focus on the acquisition of wealth: "Then Jesus said to his disciples, 'Assuredly, I say to you that it is hard for a rich man to enter the kingdom of heaven. And again I say to you, it is easier for a camel to go through the eye of a needle than for a rich man to enter the kingdom of God.'"[75] Similarly, Jesus advises us against materialism in the Sermon on the Mount:

> Do not lay up for yourselves treasures on earth, where moth and rust destroy and where thieves break in and steal; but lay up for yourselves treasures in heaven, where neither moth nor rust destroys and where thieves

do not break in and steal. For where your treasure is, there your heart will be also.[76]

His main point is crucial, that what we hold dear in our hearts determines our spiritual well-being. Material wealth itself is not the problem. The emphasis and priority we place on the acquisition of material wealth is the problem. Similarly, the apostle Paul gives explicit guidance to Timothy, "Command those who are rich in this present age not to be haughty, nor to trust in uncertain riches but in the living God, who gives us richly all things to enjoy."[77] If we trust in our material wealth to provide us happiness, our lives will remain vacant and unfulfilled; we will also suffer an eternal disconnection from God. If we trust in our spiritual connection with God to provide us happiness, we will find true pleasure in life with or without material possessions.

The American consumer economy relies on people's desire for wealth and possessions to keep it growing. Yet this encouragement of gain is directly contrary to seeking a spiritual life. Many people have recognized this contradiction, and they have sought a simpler life, divorced from consumerism. They have reduced their possessions and returned to a more spiritual existence.

However, many Americans still aspire to live in the largest house possible, where family members can be separated from one another. Television advertisements promote Internet and entertainment systems that allow each person in a home to use his or her own device without having to share. Large houses require a plethora of possessions; consequently, we spend our time, efforts, and money shopping for the best deals. These possessions all add up in value, so we protect them by living in gated communities with security systems, both of which further isolate us from our neighbors. People can't love their neighbors when they don't even know their neighbors. We live in social isolation and spiritual desolation.

To begin to change, we can acknowledge that a materialistic outlook on life is inherently wrong and recognize the vital importance of our spiritual nature. We can then look for opportunities to form spiritual connections with those around us, seek God's help and strength, and reduce our focus on material wealth. We need not feel guilty about our possessions, but as we become more spiritual, we will see our love of these possessions fade away.

Eight

Faith in Big Brother

Socialism's Destructive Effects

Socialism, a product of humanism and materialism, has historically been a spiritually destructive political force. I am referring not just to Marxist socialism, or to communism, but to all types of socialist government programs that seek to equalize the human condition. This type of socialism favors a humanistic view of mankind and the belief that each individual, with help from the state, can be improved. Each person is believed to be essentially the same. Everyone is capable of every achievement when provided with adequate education, housing, care, and sustenance. Socialism also promotes the view that all should make an equivalent effort and therefore receive identical rewards. Disparity in income is not acceptable. While this system may initially sound reasonable, experience has shown that humans do not operate well under it. The collapse of the Soviet Union and its client states in the early 1990s is just one example.

We must make a caveat here about what type of socialism we are talking about. Socialism as a pure philosophy is noble and it describes the communal life of many traditional village cultures, at least in part. Native Americans, for example, believed in sharing what they had, and they had no sense of private property rights, as far as land was concerned. The tribal members all used the land upon which they lived in common. The Democratic Socialists of America, one of today's main socialist political parties, states the current socialist position:

> Our vision of socialism is a profoundly democratic one, rooted in the belief that individuals can only reach their full potential in a society that embodies the values of liberty, equality, and solidarity. Only through creating material and cultural bonds of solidarity across racial, gender, age, national, and class lines can true equality of opportunity be achieved.[78]

Much of this position is idealistic and humane. Nevertheless, it has failed to be implemented in any meaningful way. Because our modern economic system is based on private property rights, there is no incentive for those with property to give it up to those without. Therefore, socialism has to be imposed by some power greater than that of the property owners, which has historically been the state. This state-imposed socialism is what we are critiquing here. The main problem with this type of socialism is that as the state redistributes wealth (in impersonal transactions), there is a loss of spiritual connections among people. We are not arguing that socialism in and of itself *is* necessarily bad, but that the actual implementation of state-sponsored socialism *has been* bad.

What are we arguing as the alternative? Are we defending the current global capitalistic economy as superior to socialism? No. The current globalized economy is also brutally unfair to the vast majority of people on the globe. All types of large-scale economies, capitalist or socialist, have tended to favor the powerful few. What we believe, however, is that a truly spiritual connection between people occurs when one person acts from free will to help another. If a wealthy person realizes the emptiness of his or her wealth and begins to act charitably with it, this action has a profoundly positive effect on everyone involved. If, on the other hand, the state confiscates the wealth and redistributes it under some socialist plan, this has little or no spiritual effect. It materially improves the person receiving some of the redistributed wealth, but it fails to form any spiritual connection between giver and receiver. This is the essence of the problem with government-sponsored socialism.

Government-sponsored socialism has often been materialistic, as many socialist governments have considered spirituality a form of superstition. Instead, the state assumes the role of God, attempting to control all aspects of life and set moral standards. This proves to be consistently fallible, as the members of the ruling elite tend toward corruption and destroy the state from within. Communist China's ruling elite is dealing with high-profile corruption cases as this book is being written. Judeo-Christian and Islamic beliefs clearly predict such outcomes, but this view is continuously ignored.

Socialism is a failure, even if only partially implemented, as it denies a spiritual aspect of life. Socialist policies can be applied to a small or large degree, across a spectrum. The right end of the spectrum, with only a few, minor socialist policies would accurately depict the United States at the start of the Progressive Era. The left end of the spectrum would describe China during the Cultural Revolution. Today, the United States is right of center, but gradually moving left of center. Europe has generally been left of center for the past seventy-five years. Both have failed to make the social improvements promised by socialist policy makers, such as the eradication of poverty and unemployment. Both have managed to destroy much of their countries' traditional values in the process.

Those countries that were or are far left, the hardline Communist states, have completely eradicated traditionally held values. All reports from Russia, for instance, especially after the fall of the Communist regime, show rampant amoral attitudes and a sense of a spiritual emptiness. In "Free from Morality, Or What Russia Believes In Today," Svetlana Babayeva describes how even now, Russians are grappling with what to believe and how to behave ethically.[79] Recently, Christian missionaries have had great success there, inspiring people to fill the spiritual void.

Socialist policy begins with the premise that all individuals have the right to equal wealth and social benefits. Under a purely socialist state there is no difference in standard of living, education, medical care, or housing. As wealth is generated, it is redistributed equitably. This basic premise drives all socialist policies. If socialism is introduced in a state, the first step is to redistribute the wealth by imposing more taxes and reallocating private property. The working person, then, is rewarded the same way regardless of his or her output.

In the most leftist countries, no one may own or acquire private property as well. This resembles the situation that existed in Medieval Europe for serfs, those who were essentially slaves of a landowner. Adam Smith in *The Wealth of Nations* says of the serf that "a person who can acquire no property can have no other interest but to eat as much as possible and to labour as little as possible."[80] Socialism has had exactly the same effect on worker productivity in Communist countries. Those living in public housing on welfare live by the same standard.

The effect of such policies reduces people to essentially competing for whatever limited benefits the state will pay out to them at the expense of their neighbors, who still work and pay taxes. There is no incentive to rise above this pattern of dependency because spiritually, these people have become alienated from society. Our challenge is to reach out to one another to rebuild a spiritual community.

We must note that we are not criticizing individuals who have truly suffered misfortune and been forced to turn to the state for financial assistance, such as welfare benefits or unemployment compensation. Millions of Americans are currently suffering from long-term unemployment and need help. We also understand this situation cannot be reversed overnight. Depriving these people of their only hope of subsistence would be cruel and unspiritual. What we are advocating is an eventual change to this system whereby people can freely help one another in time of need without state involvement or interference. Some may argue that this type of person-to-person assistance broke down in the past, and welfare programs came about as a result. This was true, and it was because of the very reasons we are discussing in this book. The increasing social turmoil from the Industrial Revolution to the present time has sundered spiritual connections between members of families and communities, leaving many people isolated and vulnerable to misfortune. Government-sponsored socialism has provided material relief, but it has failed to repair these connections. Our hope is that enough people begin to see the need for change, rebuild spiritual connections, and wean society off government assistance.

Since those who have wealth and property lose their gains under socialism, they tend to react against it. These "reactionaries" are persecuted by the state, as the socialist government mandates the redistribution of wealth. Where socialism is carried out lightly, such as in the United States, the opponents are taxed and pursued by the Internal Revenue Service. Where socialism is carried out heavily, such as in the Soviet Union in the early twentieth century, the reactionaries were murdered by the state. Such was the fate of millions of rich peasants, or *kulaks*, at the hands of Stalin in the 1930s, as he forced collective farming on the country. Stanford history professor Norman Naimark recently authored a book that went so far as to compare Stalin's actions with the genocide of Adolph Hitler.[81] Needless to say, this socialist campaign of devastation left survivors spiritually damaged.

Socialist governments must also set universal standards for education, healthcare, and other social benefits prior to enforcing them. This elimination of local prerogatives has developed in the United States with the formation of massive federal agencies that control much of our agriculture, education, and health. It began with Roosevelt's New Deal and has extended to today's No Child Left Behind Act and the contentious implementation of the Affordable Care Act, or "Obamacare." Removing individual and local control over these matters makes people look to the state rather than to their family or local community for guidance and protection.

Because socialism treats everyone as an economically and socially equal person, the state attempts to reeducate the populace using a combination of propaganda and fear. This reeducation is where socialism most interferes with any public discourse on spirituality. In Communist Russia or China, political prisoners were often sent to reeducation camps to learn to think in the more "enlightened" socialist way. One of the most extraordinary cases of Chinese reeducation was that of the last Emperor of China, Pu Yi, whose autobiography describes his mental change from ruler to common citizen during a ten-year incarceration.[82]

Socialist reeducation disintegrates spiritual connections between people and with God. First, it denigrates all religious beliefs, as religion recognizes a higher authority than the state, and a standard of good and evil against which the state can be judged. Socialism only can work if the state is in total control, thus religion is not a viable option. The two cannot coincide. Second, socialism works against the family, the most basic interpersonal spiritual connection, as the state must supplant parental authority and familial obligations to be effective. The state becomes the parent and provider, excluding all other actors. Inherently, the socialist goals are to produce conformity with the state's way of thinking. As this government is devoid of spirituality, interpersonal connections are precluded; each person can only truly connect with the state itself.

Socialism is generally opposed to any form of religion. Most major religions recognize that people tend to behave differently along a spectrum of good and evil. While some people are intrinsically good and others are innately unethical, most lie somewhere in between. From this standpoint, socialism is ludicrous. A short exercise in logic indicates that a socialist system will break down as the majority will tend to take advantage of socialist policies to cater to their own selfish needs. Our own experience has shown exactly that. In the United States, where socialist welfare policies were enacted in the 1960s, many people gave up working and collected welfare instead, even if they were capable of work. When welfare reform was enacted in 1996, limiting welfare benefits to five years, many of these same people magically began working again. According to both the conservative Heritage Foundation and the liberal Urban Institute, welfare caseloads were cut in half after a few years.[83] The welfare recipients used the system as long as they could for their own selfish gain until it was no longer available. Other socialist programs have a similar story.

Yet socialist policy makers believe that with more reeducation, this type of failure can be avoided. Consequently, they promote the state and its goals over religion. They do this by protecting atheism and elevating its proponents to a status equivalent with some form of religion. They oppose any religious expression in public forums. In strictly socialist countries, such as China or North Korea, religion is persecuted. In more moderately socialist areas, such as the United States and Europe, the socialists often influence religious organizations to advocate for socialist causes under the banner of "social justice." These groups push for political action within churches to advocate social equality, often raising controversy and causing division. In effect, the church's "social justice" activity puts them on the same footing as a political organization, thereby negating spirituality and instead emphasizing political action.

In contrast, Christian doctrine guides us to pray, seek answers in Scripture, and ask the Holy Spirit to guide our actions in the face of a controversy. However, social justice committees tend to ignore this basic doctrine and instead focus on demonstrations and public advocacy. The church then becomes a tool for enacting socialist policies and God is left as a bystander. All of this political action often leaves church members confused and divided, further impeding their abilities to connect.

Many church members may feel this criticism is too harsh. Social justice committees are generally made up of good people trying to do the right thing. Nevertheless, the basic premise under which these committees operate is that church members must unite and fight against some sort of injustice. This is a humanistic and socialist approach, and it is neither Christian nor spiritual. It places hope in politics, not in God. Jesus never advocated political action against injustice. He did not call for people to rally or demonstrate. Instead, he said, "love your enemies, bless those who curse you, do good to those who hate you, and pray for those who spitefully use you and persecute you." [84] He knew that by having one person love another, God's spiritual power would spread and correct these injustices naturally, as spiritual connections grew. Modern churches, many of which suffer declining membership, could revive themselves by following this simple example and rejecting humanism and socialism.

Socialism's greatest competitor is the family, as children are born with an innate connection to their parents. In an effort to counteract this bond, socialist policies undermine all aspects of family life by having the state assume the role of parent and provider. Parental authority is challenged in many ways by socialism. In hardline communist countries, state agents would often separate children from parents and brainwash them to have them turn in their own mothers or fathers. This was the horrific fate for many Cambodians under the Khmer Rouge. As one survivor describes,

> They [the Khmer Rouge] encouraged children to find fault with their own parents and spy on them. They openly showed their intention to destroy the family structure that once held love, faith, comfort, happiness, and companionship. They took young children from their homes to live in a commune so that they could indoctrinate them.[85]

In countries with more moderate socialism, such as in Europe and the United States, parents are often overruled by the state. Some American states allow minors to purchase contraception without parental authority, and some even allow abortions. Some states also make it illegal for teachers or school staff members who learn of a teen pregnancy from telling the teen's parents without her consent. The reason given for these measures is to protect the child; the unspoken assumption is that the state is a better guardian than the parents. The socialist state's war on parenthood is merely enacted in an effort to belittle a competing authority and convince children of state supremacy.

Another aspect of the socialist destruction of the family is the state's attempt to take over familial obligations. In the United States, Social Security, Medicare, and Medicaid have reduced filial obligations to care for elderly parents. While many people still do care for their parents, many opt to let their parents live alone or in a nursing home where Social Security and Medicaid pay the bills. Similarly, all forms of government assistance, from welfare to food stamps to unemployment compensation make the state the primary agent of reliability. Before these programs were in place, people primarily relied on family and friends. While such support was often materially inferior to what the state can provide today, it was the support by one person for another. It was a personal transaction, and it kept people spiritually connected with one another.

Bryan: My father remembers that as a boy in Vermont, on any visit to someone's farm, a grandparent or other older relative was usually in the home. These people lived with their children or relatives at the end of their lives, often contributing to the family workload. Sometimes, they were a burden on the family, too. Nevertheless, the young children and other family members knew this older person and connected with them right to the end. More recently, my mother's mother lived out her life in a small apartment attached to her older son's house. She remained part of the immediate family all of her life.

Even now, I know many people who have decided to care for an elderly family member. While today's nursing homes or assisted living facilities can offer better accommodations and medical care, are these benefits worth the cost in separating ourselves from one another? It is an intensely personal choice how best to handle this situation. I only suggest that we all think about what is truly important. If one believes that life on earth is only an interlude in our spiritual eternity, then remaining connected with family members is far more important than extending one's life for a brief period in an isolated state of existence. *~End~*

China exemplifies a radical change in this tradition as a result of extremely strict socialist policies, coupled with its expanding global economy. Prior to communism, China's traditional society was based on family, as it followed Confucian principles. In *China as I See It*, Pearl S. Buck describes how Chinese families felt a deep obligation to care for all their members and how it was a severe disgrace against the family if one of its members was neglected.[86] There was no insurance, other than what the family could provide for one another. With the state as a safety net, people now can take on less responsibility for one another. This degradation of support and compassion distances people from each other and harms their relationships.

While many Chinese continue to maintain strong family ties and care for one another, there is a growing problem in China with children neglecting their elderly parents. In July 2013, the Chinese government actually enacted legislation mandating that children show more care for their parents. As Xia Xueluan, professor of social studies at Peking University, explains, "In the past, just a few people treated their parents badly, but now there's a large group of Chinese who are un-filial, so it's necessary to legislate to protect the rights of the elderly and promote moral integrity."[87] Such is the effect of socialism and globalization in China.

Socialism is a highly destructive force that hinders or even prohibits the open attempt of people to connect spiritually with God or with one another. How should we face this threat? We can look to the early Christian Church for an example to follow. Under the Roman Empire, it suffered far worse persecution than we do today, but it grew quickly and continuously until the empire itself became Christian. Following this example, we must work in cooperation with each other and develop a relationship with God however we can, despite any meddling from the state. This approach is far more helpful than the fruitless course of political action or social justice.

The other action we can each take is to seek ways to help one another, rather than seek help from the state as "victims." For example, we can do whatever we can to help a friend who has lost his or her job. Such a person will feel humiliated and despondent at first. Imagine the change in his or her feelings if friends and family gathered around and helped find some sort of replacement income or employment. Additionally, if the unemployed person were to forego seeking government assistance and instead rely on his or her friends and family, imagine the gratitude and close bonds of friendship that could result. Materially, everyone might end up worse off than if the unemployed person had sought assistance from the state, but spiritually, all involved will benefit.

Bryan: I know my paternal grandfather lost his job in the Barre, Vermont granite quarries at the height of the Great Depression. He survived this personal disaster because of friends and family, as unemployment insurance did not exist. He was employed part-time by a family member who had a farm, and he was helped by friends in Barre who secured him a job that paid less, but helped him make ends meet. According to my father, his father retained his dignity and remained connected to society through this ordeal, thanks to the support around him. How different for someone today who is essentially ostracized by unemployment and only gets the cold, bureaucratic response of the state through unemployment checks. I am not criticizing anyone who has had to take unemployment compensation, but only pointing out that it does nothing for someone spiritually. *~End~*

Nine

Surviving the Invasion

Globalization's Destructive Effects

Globalization is a rapidly accelerating economic and social force that began in the Age of Exploration and progressed during the Industrial Revolution. Now it is the means by which the information society economy spreads around the globe. Globalization is the product of materialism, as it prioritizes material acquisition and commercial expansion above all else. Globalization has also evolved from capitalism to become the primary economic force in the world. We are in a post-capitalist society, as Peter Drucker has explained. Capitalism is a system where capital flows freely to whoever can use it most productively. It is an unspiritual system, as its main premise is that individual greed is the prime motivation of economic activity, and the free market, an economic exchange with no restrictions, is the prime determinant of supply and demand. Compassion and empathy are antithetical to the capitalist system. Globalization on the other hand is a system where immense capital is controlled closely by global financial powers. Large financial firms, exemplified by Wall Street in the United States, are constantly seeking a better return on their investments, regardless of social consequences. For example, most multinational corporations in the United States have invested in vast commercial operations with communist China, regardless of the effects on both American and Chinese society. The global corporations' only interest is to maximize their income stream.

Globalization has also had a virtual aspect in the information society revolution. Thomas Friedman describes the world as getting "flatter," as the computer and the Internet allow an unprecedented and increasing global exchange of information. [88] This global interchange of information is replacing the global exchange of capital as the most important economic activity as we become an information society. The result of this global access to information is that foreign competition undercuts the efforts of local business in providing information or services.

Globalization has had a destructive social effect on various cultures around the world. As the global economic superpowers, especially the United States, have pushed to open markets in different countries, they have also flooded those countries with consumer goods and services that are alien to the native cultures. Western clothing, Hollywood movies, and American popular music can now be found almost anywhere on earth. For the recipient nations, this wave of foreign culture has inundated their own cultures and drowned their native customs. According to the World Health Organization, "There are many debates about whether globalization increases or reduces cultural diversity or homogenization. For many, the influences of Western culture through TV, cinema advertising, radio, etc., are substituting for and competing with local and minority cultures."[89] Fragile cultures often do not survive this invasion.

Global free trade now requires that the cheapest source of production is favored over any local or national desire to retain the production of a particular good or service. Textiles, automobiles, call centers, and even scientific research are all becoming global commodities whose production moves more and more frequently to the cheapest producer. This trend has tarnished the connection between employers and employees, as there is little or no job security. As employers can more readily threaten to send jobs overseas to cheaper labor pools, workers have given in to whatever demands the employers make. As a result, employees are often embittered toward their employers, as they feel exploited instead of valued. Traditional labor unions have been ineffective in dealing with this trend. A better approach is for each employee to face this challenge and seek connections with fellow employees, gradually building a spiritual network of support. Employers can also help change this situation by dealing with employees openly and fairly, perhaps sacrificing some profits for the sake of their organization's spiritual health.

Another effect of global free trade is a very transient labor force, as people readily travel to new job locations. This nomadic tendency does not help people form spiritual connections. Strong ties to people, the land, and its traditions require time to develop, and continuous movement is not conducive to such relationships. Under globalization, people move around more and more and lose their ties to any particular place. How this affects one's spiritual life is unclear, but many cultures affirm the importance of a tie to the land upon which one lives.

Bryan: I grew up on Cape Cod, and while I moved around during my military career, I yearned to go back and visit the beaches and back roads I had known as a child. Today, I still return and feel a deep connection with these places. They are natural places of beauty, and I never tire of them. Our modern, transient society and characterless suburban or urban environments do nothing to help us spiritually, and often rob us of part of our spiritual background. If we can, we may find some spiritual solace in rebuilding a link with the land, wherever it may be.

In 2013, I attended a public conversation with Wendell Berry, a writer, philosopher, and agricultural activist, sponsored by the Yale University Chubb Fellowship. He also advocated a care for the land upon which we live, and the spiritual dimension of land stewardship. We could follow his advice by connecting with others and finding ways to care for the land around us. Today's urban gardeners are one example we could follow, as they have brought people together who share in the nurturing of a plot of land to grow food right in the midst of a city. Not only does the land benefit, but the community also grows closer and more spiritual. *~End~*

Americans' loss of common knowledge and skills is yet another effect of globalization. Globalization eliminates all jobs in a given region, except for those that are still competitive on a global scale. Occasionally, an American town or city can retain some key industrial or agricultural jobs, but most have been deemed noncompetitive and are now performed overseas in a cheaper labor pool. Furthermore, as Christopher Lasch points out in "Degradation of the Practical Arts," "Over and over again, new technologies have reduced even the engineer's work to a routine. What originates as a craft degenerates into a series of automated operations performed more or less unthinkingly."[90]

All that remains are jobs in local services and the public sector. Even these careers are competing to sustain their existence. This results in a depletion of specific jobs that require deep skill sets such as farmers, craftsmen, machinists, doctors, bakers, and butchers. Now one finds a few superficially trained service providers, usually in some national or global franchise, such as a cook in a fast food restaurant. This deficiency in common knowledge drives people to buy cheap global products or services instead of finding their own solutions. This causes a break in the spiritual connection people once felt with their past, with their ancestors, and with their community.

Globalization stretches and breaks the connection between the producer and the consumer, as people purchase things with complete ignorance of their origins. However, this ignorance is not necessarily the consumer's fault; it is often difficult to determine where a product comes from. Automobiles, for example, are made from parts from all over the world, and may be assembled in the United States or overseas. Even food has become globalized. Beef today may come from the United States, Australia, Argentina, or Brazil. The person eating it has no affiliation with the cattle or farmers involved. Contrast this situation with that of a person who goes to a local farmer's market and buys produce from the person who grew it. The connection in the latter case is much stronger as it involves physically meeting and interacting with another human being, a human being who put time and effort into providing you with that meal. The rapid growth of the locally grown food market is evidence that people feel better buying food from a person they know and who they can reward directly for producing organic food in a sustainable way. The connections made between the farmer and consumer and the connections between humans and the animals or produce consumed are all potentially spiritual.

Finally, Capra points out that globalization has not uniformly connected people, but only connected the economically viable parts of the population:

> Global capitalism has increased poverty and social inequality not only by transforming the relationships between capital and labor, but also through the process of "social exclusion," which is a direct consequence of the new economy's network structure. As the flows of capital and information interlink worldwide networks, they exclude from these networks all populations and territories that are of no value or interest to their search for financial gain."[91]

Therefore, globalization, while touted as a way of connecting people around the globe, is really a selective network of the cheapest goods and services to the busiest markets, at the exclusion of all else. It is highly destructive to spiritual connections among people, as it is the ultimate in a "survival of the fittest" system. Poor mill towns and cities exemplify this trend. Globalization repeatedly causes formerly prosperous industrial centers to collapse under high rates of unemployment, excessive public welfare, and crime. For instance, in Detroit, a once prosperous industrial world power, many areas of the city are currently being plowed under and returned to empty land. In this situation, people are left hopeless, mistrusting of others, and consequently skeptical of God. Only a strong trust in God can help us face this challenge.

Bryan: One practical thing we can do is to treat our local businesses and their owners with compassion. We can seek ways to buy locally made products or locally provided services. We may pay more, but if we make a personal connection with the business owner, it's worth it. Our spiritual connections within our community should include all people with whom we have contact. Business people should count. If we connect with them, we improve our own spirituality, we improve their spirituality, and we help their businesses.

My family and I have developed a strong bond with a family that runs a restaurant in our town. We have gotten to know the owners and have eaten there regularly for years. Each time we go, we spend time talking with them and catch up on one another's family stories. We occasionally bring them a gift, usually something my wife has made, and in return, the owners treat us to free desserts occasionally. While we could search and perhaps find a slightly better place in terms of food or ambiance, we return to this place over and over because of the connection we feel to the owners. This connection goes far deeper than the quality of the food or service. It is truly spiritual, and it helps us and them. *~End~*

Ten

Life in the Big City

Urbanization's Destructive Effects

Urbanization is another economic and social force that has grown in today's information society and globalized economy. Urbanization is the process in which people move from the countryside to the city. It has been cyclical throughout history, but we are currently in an accelerated trend toward urbanization on a scale unseen in the past. According to the United Nations:

> The world is undergoing the largest wave of urban growth in history. In 2008, for the first time in history, more than half of the world's population will be living in towns and cities. By 2030 this number will swell to almost 5 billion, with urban growth concentrated in Africa and Asia. While mega-cities have captured much public attention, most of the new growth will occur in

smaller towns and cities, which have fewer resources to respond to the magnitude of the change...Poverty is now growing faster in urban than in rural areas. One billion people live in urban slums, which are typically overcrowded, polluted and dangerous, and lack basic services such as clean water and sanitation.[92]

Urbanization generally hurts and hinders spiritual connections. Outside of cities, people traditionally lived in rural communities, either as nomadic tribes in a particular territory or as villagers farming a particular region. People in these rural communities had many spiritual connections. They felt a connection to the land where they lived. Anyone who has farmed, or even gardened, understands this connection. This spiritual connection extended to obtaining food, either by hunting, raising animals, or growing crops. The Native Americans, for example, felt a spiritual connection with the animals they hunted, and they respected them as fellow creatures on the earth. As just discussed, how many of us feel such a spiritual connection when we eat a hamburger today?

People in rural communities also felt a connection with one another. Members of a nomadic tribe or a village all knew one another and often were related in some way. They also knew that they lived or died as a unitary organization. The individual had rights, but the rights of the tribe or village took precedence. If it was hunting time, or harvest time, all able bodied adults took part. Similarly, if one person was sick or hurt, the others took care of him or her, understanding that others would do the same for them.

Finally, people in rural communities typically had strong traditions, connecting them spiritually with their ancestors. Traditions took the form of beliefs, customs, music, festivals, and other activities that had been passed down from one generation to the next. In all these things, rural people enjoyed a level of spiritual connection unknown to city dwellers.

Many people today live in what are called "rural communities," but these are often far different than what was just described. Today's rural communities are often isolated houses on large lots, or spread out sub-divisions. The community spirit in these rural areas can vary widely, and people often feel isolated from one another. Frequently, in idyllic areas, such as parts of New England, many rural homes are owned by out-of-towners who only visit periodically. Rarely do these communities resemble a traditional village. Thus, neither the amount of development present in a community, nor its classification as rural, suburban, or urban is the real issue. What is important are the spiritual ties felt among the residents.

Bryan: I felt a semblance of a traditional rural community's spiritual connections when we lived in England. We quickly searched for a house on arrival in the country and settled on a three-hundred-year old converted cottage in Feltwell, a rural village outside of one of the US air bases. It was in a quiet corner of East Anglia that had escaped most modern development. We became involved in the village, as we sent our two boys to the village schools, attended church in the village, and made friends there. What struck us was the far slower and quieter pace of life compared to our life in American towns or cities. Each year, the village had a cycle of small festivals and events, and many of the inhabitants took part. One of our favorite times was before Christmas when the ancient village church held a carol service. The church had no seats or pews, so everyone stood, and we sang a cappella. The tradition had gone on for decades, and everyone participating felt a special bond. I never felt a stronger sense of the Christmas spirit before or since. *~End~*

When a person moves to a city, he or she usually loses most or all of these spiritual connections. He or she is physically separated from the land and instead has the city, with its filth and pollution as his or her new abode. There is little desire to connect with it. The connection with food is lost, as the closest connection one has with what one eats is the marketplace. People in cities are also isolated from one another and share little common purpose, as each pursues his or her own livelihood, independent of others. Finally, traditions are obliterated in cities where everyone comes from different places with different customs and beliefs. In some cases, neighborhoods grow with people of similar backgrounds, but these do not last for more than a generation or two. Little Italy in New York City, for example, is a shadow of what it was fifty years ago. What replaces the old traditions is new ones that tend to be shallow and less fulfilling, such as the link with the city's sports teams. Even these connections have become tenuous as the team owners and players jump from city to city to chase the highest possible revenue.

This isolation that people feel in cities also gives them a sense of anonymity and increases the propensity for wrongdoing and even crime. People feel less inhibited when they think nobody knows what they are doing. This makes cities generally more dangerous than the countryside. As a result, people in cities are less trusting and less likely to reach out to others, even if they appear in need. This mistrust caused by urbanization is one of the primary impediments to a spiritual life.

Why is urbanization occurring at an increasing pace if it is detrimental to a spiritual life and to making spiritual connections? There are three reasons. First, as globalization increases, there are fewer and fewer areas of prosperity, and these tend to attract people for economic reasons. As the people flow there, cities grow. Second, the state has found that a few large agricultural producers provide a better export market income than many small producers can provide, so small producers are pushed off the land and must move to the cities. Third, the state has found that an urbanized population is much easier to influence and control than a rural population. While we are not advocating any political action against urbanization, we think it is important to understand the trend for what it is.

Globalization has further concentrated populations into urban agglomerations. Not all cities share in this growth; only the ones that are globally competitive do. In a keynote address for the "South Asia Urban and City Management Course" at the World Bank Institute, Dr. Yue-man Yeung of The Chinese University of Hong Kong explains:

> Globalization is a multifaceted process of drawing countries, cities and people ever closer together through increasing flows of people, goods, capital, services and ideas. Certain cities, namely, world cities, have come to the fore because of the special functions they perform in the new global economy, with an emphasis on the refined division of labour and comparative advantage.[93]

In other words, some cities coming "to the fore" means that others are left behind. Many cities decay, such as the American Rust Belt cities, while a few grow, such as New York, Mumbai, and Shanghai, as they remain or become competitive. With fewer places of prosperity, people face the choice of moving to one of the few competitive cities or remaining poor in the countryside or in a passed-over city. Mobility makes spiritual connections difficult, as everyone becomes transitory. Moving around breaks up families and friendships. If a person is moving around on his or her own, then only God can remain a constant, ever-present connection.

State agricultural policies have encouraged rural depopulation to make way for larger, more economically efficient farm producers, causing more urbanization in the process. This trend started with the Enclosure Acts in England from the 16th to the 19th century when commoners were bought off and moved to villages or towns to allow large landowners to consolidate all their small plots of farmland. According to *The Land* magazine, "Britain set out, more or less deliberately, to become a highly urbanized economy with a large urban proletariat dispossessed from the countryside, highly concentrated landownership, and farms far larger than any other country in Europe."[94] This urbanization benefited a few wealthy proprietors at the expense of vast numbers of dispossessed rural poor.

The same trend has happened in the United States, where factory farms have largely replaced the family farm, depopulating and impoverishing rural areas. The Economist states, "For the past two years the total population of rural America has fallen for the first time since the Census Bureau began tracking it in the 1970's...The majority of rural counties— 1261 out of a total of 1976—had shrinking headcounts."[95] The article goes on to describe how smaller numbers of farmers and farm workers have led to fewer businesses in nearby towns; the rural economy has contracted. The trend continues in developing countries. As explained in a study by the University of Michigan,

> In order to produce agricultural products quickly, efficiently, and for a decent price, national governments often look to decrease the number of small producers, and turn agricultural production and resource extraction over to larger enterprises, with larger production facilities, and a lower per-unit cost of production.[96]

The most recent example of this trend is in India, where the government has begun to allow large agribusiness ventures in the country. One major goal of the Indian government is the "consolidation of holdings all over the country."[97] This is the same policy followed since the Enclosure Acts, and despite any government efforts to protect small farmers, the predictable result will be rural depopulation.

Wendell Berry, an outspoken advocate for rural communities and farming, has pointed out the social destruction that accompanies industrial-scale farming and rural depopulation. In a lecture sponsored by the National Endowment for the Humanities, he explains:

> Industrialists and industrial economists have assumed, with permission from the rest of us, that land and people can be divorced without harm. If farmers come under adversity from high costs and low prices, then

they must either increase their demands upon the land and decrease their care for it, or they must sell out and move to town, and this is supposed to involve no ecological or economic or social cost. Or if there are such costs, then they are rated as "the price of progress" or "creative destruction." But land abuse cannot brighten the human prospect. There is in fact no distinction between the fate of the land and the fate of the people. When one is abused, the other suffers.[98]

It is clear that urbanization and the destruction of rural livelihoods have a profoundly negative effect on the people forced to migrate to cities and on their spiritual state.

Maggie: A general lack of concern and acknowledgment for the environment has become increasingly apparent to me. In this day in age, it amazes me that we continue to litter our earth. What troubles me even more, is when blatantly recyclable items, such as water bottles, end up in garbage cans that are placed just under ten feet from bright blue recycling bins. Are we all in such a rush? Or are we simply indifferent? I don't think we are aware of the colossal impact we have on the environment. Urbanization has distanced us from nature; few of us are truly cognizant of how critical our environment is in every aspect of our lives. As we continually emphasize and prioritize the building of new infrastructure and the profits it brings, we compromise vital ecosystems that are necessary to sustain life, natural resources, and an equilibrium. *~End~*

The final cause for urbanization is the state's desire to control its population. The Industrial Revolution caused the explosive growth of cities in the West and resulted in our present day urban landscape. As industries expanded and demanded labor, people were enticed out of rural communities to work for higher pay in the cities, with none of the cares of the farm. At first, the state was a spectator in this process and even viewed the growing urban population as a threat. The "mob" was feared and suppressed by the state. In Victorian London, the city became a nightmarish hell for its poorest residents who lived in crime infested *rookeries.*

Soon, however, the state realized that an urban population is much easier to control for some simple reasons. Urban populations are concentrated, so police can oversee them more easily. Historically, if an uprising occurred, it was easier to quell it in an urban environment, than in a rural one.[99] Urban populations are much more dependent on others to survive, as growing one's own food or making one's own household items becomes virtually impossible in a city. The urban population is also much easier to influence, whether through mass education or mass communication. For all these reasons, the state has learned to appreciate the advantages of an urban population.

In the United States and other countries with representative governments, politicians learned to use urban populations for their political gain. City political bosses, able to rally thousands of urban voters, became the nation's power brokers. In turn, these bosses doled out political favors and money to stay in power. This system continues today in a modified form, as politicians have assumed the role of the bosses. These politicians maintain their power base in their cities by promising government assistance in exchange for votes. The problem these politicians are facing today is that the system is going bankrupt. Once the money stops flowing in to support the urban poor, the state will lose control of them. This happened in the former communist countries of Eastern Europe. It is happening in the European Union today in places like Greece and Spain. It is starting to happen in the United States in cities like Detroit, which recently declared bankruptcy.

A new model for urbanized population control can be seen in China. The Chinese Communists long had trouble controlling their vast population, which was mostly rural. Chinese peasants had strong families and strong communities, as discussed earlier. The Chinese Communists witnessed the decay of the Soviet Union during the 1970s, and they realized they had to change to survive. Therefore, they began to allow capitalist ventures, first on a small scale, then on a larger scale, primarily in rural areas. The Chinese economy began to take off.

However, as Yasheng Huang describes in *Capitalism with Chinese Characteristics*, the Communist regime felt things had gone too far by 1989 with the demonstrations in Tiananmen

Square, so it cracked down on the entrepreneurial capitalists. Instead, the state began to take over the capitalist ventures and brought them into the cities where the state had more control. As a result, China's economy today is dominated by urban, state-owned companies.[100] These companies entice the rural poor to come to the cities and work. These people lose their connections with their rural lifestyle and become urbanized and more controllable. They also are more materialistic, seeking happiness from consumer goods, much like people in the West. At the same time, the state officials overseeing the companies grow rich from the state enterprises, often through corrupt business practices. The old Confucian traditions and associated spiritual connections are extinguished.

Americans are generally witless accomplices to the urbanization of China's and other developing nations' populations. In China, we provide the capital to the state-owned enterprises by consuming Chinese goods at an increasing rate. At the same time, we pretend to think the Chinese are becoming more like us. We fail to see that the Chinese Communist Party is one of the most ruthless and successful regimes in history, and it will not jeopardize its own power by liberating its economy or its population. In other developing countries, we have no idea what type of conditions the urban workers are in, but we gladly buy the cheap merchandise they sell us. Occasionally, a sad story will briefly get our attention about slave-like conditions at a foreign factory or a horrific accident at another. Therefore, each of us must look at the facts and decide how best to spend his or her own money without supporting this trend toward urbanization. If not, then we are furthering the spiritual disconnects that urbanization causes.

We can also examine ourselves and ask honestly what we expect from life. If we are seeking materialistic gain, then supporting the advance of urbanization makes sense. But if we want a more spiritual life, connected to those around us and to the land upon which we live, then we can make choices that support the people and land around us. We do not need to become political activists. Instead, we can just begin to think and act more deliberately. We can support local businesses and farms. We can get involved in our local communities. We can live a lifestyle that involves less consumption and more renewal. The first step is to find others who want to attain these goals and connect with them. The next step is to begin to think for ourselves, rejecting the materialistic propaganda of politicians and corporations. Eventually, we can begin to form a better society of spiritually connected people who realize the detriments of uncontrolled urbanization and quietly work to reverse it.

Eleven

All Alone

Symptoms of Spiritual Disconnection

Human suffering is increasing. We see an increase in the suffering of individuals and in the suffering of groups of people. According to the Judeo-Christian worldview, suffering occurs because of the original sin of Adam that separated humankind from God. According to Islam, it occurs because of unbelievers. According to Zen Buddhism, it occurs because of bad *karma*. According to Native American beliefs, it occurs because of a violation of harmony with the spiritual world. In all these faiths, spiritual disconnection is the root cause of suffering. What we are seeing today is a rise in suffering all over the globe unlike any seen in the past, and all faiths indicate that this increase is due to the fact that more people than ever before are spiritually disconnected. Yet modern commentators almost never mention a lack of spirituality as a factor in this suffering.

One effect of the spiritual disconnection seen in many people is a general feeling of isolation and discontent, sometimes to the point of mental illness. The information society and globalization are rapidly changing the economy and society. As people move in and out of jobs and in and out of communities more and more, they no longer have time to make the social contacts they once did. Instead, they feel alone. A study in Germany concluded:

> Our analysis demonstrated that measures of social isolation in neighbourhoods and social contacts at work influenced admission for schizophrenia and depression: in neighbourhoods with less social contacts and with a higher proportion of persons not working the admission rates increased.[101]

As people have felt increasingly isolated or disconnected from others, their mental health has suffered. Another study showed that despite all the advances made by the feminist movement, women also show signs of increased unhappiness over the past four decades. [102] The authors of the article describing this increase had no explanation. In both articles, there was no mention of spirituality. What else explains this discontent?

Human suffering has been most apparent in the rise of suicide rates. According to the Centers for Disease Control, beginning in 2010, deaths in the United States due to suicide exceeded those due to car accidents for the first time. There were 38,364 suicides, compared to 33,687 motor vehicle deaths. [103] Suicide rates typically have been highest among teenagers and the elderly, but in this case, the big rise was among middle-aged Americans:

> From 1999 to 2010, the suicide rate among Americans ages 35 to 64 rose by nearly 30 percent, to 17.6 deaths per 100,000 people, up from 13.7. Although suicide rates are growing among both middle-aged men and women, far more men take their own lives. The suicide rate for middle-aged men was 27.3 deaths per 100,000, while for women it was 8.1 deaths per 100,000...The most pronounced increases were seen among men in their 50's, a group in which suicide rates jumped by nearly 50 percent, to about 30 per 100,000. For women, the largest increase was seen in those ages 60 to 64, among whom rates increased by nearly 60 percent, to 7.0 per 100,000. [104]

There was no clear explanation given for this increase, other than mentioning that it correlated with an increase in Americans' use of prescription pain-killers and anti-depressants. There was no mention of spirituality. But if we consider the demographic group showing the most increase in suicides, the Baby Boomer generation, and especially men in their fifties, we realize that this group has been the most adversely affected by the information society and globalization. According to Dr. Julie Phillips, an associate professor of sociology at Rutgers University who has studied suicide rates, "'The boomers had great expectations for what their life might look like, but I think perhaps it hasn't panned out that way,' due to changes in marriage, social isolation and family roles."[105]

In other words, these people, raised under the philosophies of humanism and materialism, tried to build lives of their own making, aiming for happiness derived from success at work, the accumulation of wealth, and worldly gain. However, as King Solomon learned, all this was just "grasping for the wind,"[106] and left many of them feeling empty. Instead, they encountered the whirlwind changes wrought by the information society's new economy, and many of them became unexpectedly unemployed or sidelined in their careers. In many cases they were left in financial straits. Additionally, the social changes occurring left them bewildered. They no longer felt that they were part of a community or a society that they understood. They were already spiritually disconnected in many cases, but now they were also socially disconnected. Such isolation breeds despair, and in many cases, suicide.

Bryan: I am in this demographic group, and I have seen firsthand what this study shows. My age group was raised to be self-sufficient and to "play by the rules" in order to succeed. We were coached to be loyal to our organizations and to be productive members by working hard. What many of us have seen, however, is that modern corporations have jettisoned employees with little compunction in order to maintain high profits and shareholder returns. Many employees felt betrayed. As retired military officer and as a public school teacher, I have seen this trend creeping into the public sector as government leaders seek quick ways to solve financial problems. The result is that older men feel that the world has shifted and left them behind. The same men are often psychologically ill-equipped to seek help, even from friends and family. Everyone around such men needs to recognize that they feel desperate, even if they don't show it, so they need help and support. There is no better antidote than human compassion and prayer for these men and for others like them who feel betrayed and alone. *~End~*

Worldwide, suicide now claims more lives than war, natural disasters, and murder, with most of the suicides occurring in developed countries. [107] Dr. Thomas Joiner, a researcher and professor of psychology at Florida State University developed a theory that suicide requires three overlapping conditions: "thwarted belongingness," or a sense of being socially isolated; "perceived burdensomeness," or a sense of uselessness and being a burden to others; and "capability for suicide," or not fearing death. When a person feels all three conditions strongly, he or she is at risk for suicide.[108]

Joiner could not quantitatively measure the first condition, involving a sense of belonging, but qualitatively speaking, he found that it related to interpersonal connections. He noted that twins and mothers of small children were at the lowest risk of suicide while those people who had never married or had divorced were at a much higher risk. The second condition, perceiving oneself as a burden, typically afflicted those who felt they imposed on others, such as the unemployed or terminally ill. The third condition, not fearing death, depended on a person's background, especially his or her experience with death or violence in the past. He does not mention spirituality as a factor anywhere. Yet we can see that reaching out and spiritually connecting with a person who felt these three conditions would certainly help give them a sense of "belongingness" and reduce any sense of "burdensomeness."

Social isolation is the subject of the book, *Bowling Alone*, in which Robert Putnam shares data from almost five-hundred-thousand interviews of various people. He found that social connections among people had drastically declined over the past few decades so that people no longer did things together or belonged to groups as they once had, including bowling leagues. People preferred to bowl alone now. [109] Putnam focuses on membership in organized groups, and the trend he sees is a big drop in numbers. He points out that about half of all group memberships are in some sort of religious institution. He does not emphasize the spirituality of these social connections, but many of them had to be spiritual. Any group of people sharing a fun or challenging experience tends to bond and form spiritual connections.

Another symptom of society's spiritual disconnection is the increase in violence, especially in brutal acts against helpless victims. School shootings have been the most stunning. *Slate Magazine* reporter Chris Kirk explains that, "There have been a total of 137 fatal school shootings that killed 297 victims since 1980. Elementary schools saw the fewest shootings (17), while high schools saw the most (62). Each decade had more shooting deaths than the previous one."[110] After each shooting, the public discourse is vehement for more gun control and other measures to stop future shootings. Schools implement more security and zero-tolerance measures against weapons on school grounds. Nevertheless, the number of shootings continues to increase.

Maggie: I was six on September 11, 2001, when 2,996 people died in the attacks on the World Trade Center and the Pentagon Building. I've been jaded by violence. Fifteen people were killed in 1999 at Columbine High School. Thirty-two people were murdered at Virginia Tech in 2007. Twelve people died in 2012 at a movie theatre in Aurora, Colorado. Twenty-seven people lost their lives in 2012 at Sandy Hook Elementary School. These shootings were horrific and despicable. But, shocking? No. My generation is accustomed to the ruthless killing of innocent students and civilians. It's just something that happens, neither appalling nor out of the ordinary. They're travesties, atrocious and devastating. Nevertheless, they have seemingly become an annual occurrence; their frequency has distorted our perspective. They are another tragic news story that brews an impassioned gun debate within our country. They are a part of the society I grew up in. Deplorable? Yes. Abnormal? No. ~*End*~

The Centers for Disease Control's Division of Adolescent and School Violence has studied school violence for the past twenty years. This organization promotes certain measures that have proved to reduce school violence such as "universal, school-based prevention programs" that promote social skills, including "conflict resolution and teamwork;" "parent- and family-based programs;" and "mentoring programs" that "pair a young person with an adult who can serve as a positive role model."[111] All of these measures provide positive interpersonal connections and could be considered spiritual, though that quality is never mentioned.

We should not believe that this problem of school violence is new, requiring some sort of new solution. Violence is an age-old problem that all major faiths associate with spiritual disconnection. The Bible is replete with examples. After the fall of humankind and the introduction to sin into the world, "the earth also was corrupt before God, and the earth was filled with violence."[112] Later, Solomon states that the "wicked," (Hebrew word, *rasha*, meaning *morally wrong* or *ungodly*)[113] "drink the wine of violence."[114] Just before the fall of Jerusalem to the Babylonians, the prophet Ezekiel receives a vision from God. Ezekiel witnesses the Jewish religious leaders secretly performing abominable and idolatrous ceremonies in the Jewish temple, thereby insulting God. God says of the Jewish leaders that "they have filled the land with violence."[115]

In all these quotes, the word *violence* is a translation of the Hebrew word *chamac*, meaning *violence from injustice and cruelty*, not from a natural disaster or some other random event. The *Holman Illustrated Bible Dictionary* explains that violence (*chamac*) is equated with sin, a separation from God, and that it results in a "cold-blooded and unscrupulous infringement of the personal rights of others, motivated by greed and hate and often making use of physical violence and brutality."[116] This sounds like the description of a typical school shooting.

All news accounts of the home of the shooter in the Newtown tragedy, Adam Lanza, point to a socially isolated individual who became spiritually desolate and suicidal. He apparently played violent video games by himself in the basement of a large house in a wealthy neighborhood and rarely saw anyone else. His only contact with his mother was through e-mail, even though they lived in the same house. These factors alone would not account for the horrific nature of his crime, but they certainly did not help him spiritually connect with anyone. When we really think about this crime, we need to ask how it could have happened. The news media latched on to possible issues with mental health care and gun control, but missed the mark.

The central issue was that Lanza had lost all spiritual connection with other human beings and with God, as seen by his willingness to shoot and kill his mother, twenty young children, six school staff, and himself. He was an extreme case, but also a more and more common case of how spiritual disconnection can be manifested. This deadly manifestation is warned against in the Bible, in the Islamic Koran, in Zen Buddhism, and in most other faiths. They all affirm that a lack of spirituality is an unbalanced state that leads to evil thoughts and evil actions. We must realize that this situation is anything but normal. It cries out for action. And so we must act by building spiritual connections and saving one another from this rise in evil and suffering.

Just as individuals have become spiritually isolated, so have groups or communities felt the same sort of spiritual isolation and manifested the same sort of unbalanced thoughts and actions. The most notorious such groups are today's terrorists. However, terrorism is the symptom, not the disease. Every group that has employed terrorism has done so out of desperation, as they felt isolated and powerless against other groups arrayed against them.

But here we have to make a caveat, as many isolated groups of people in history have not used terrorism as a weapon against their perceived enemies. For example, the early Christians in the Roman Empire remained nonviolent and generally passive in the face of Roman persecution. More recently, the vast majority of African Americans working for civil rights in the United States used nonviolent demonstrations and protests. What makes one group nonviolent while another resorts to terrorism? The nonviolent groups have had a spiritual connection with God and with one another, despite their feeling of being spiritually disconnected from their opposition, while the violent ones have lost their spiritual connection with God and with other people.

This difference in spirituality is the only logical explanation for the difference in behavior. Dr. Martin Luther King, Jr. and his followers used nonviolence in the face of racist lynching, fire hoses, and police dogs. Today's terrorists, even when treated decently as new immigrants or citizens in the United States or Europe, have used bombs and suicide attacks against their fellow countrymen. Why? Because Dr. King had a spiritual connection with God and with his fellow civil rights advocates that strengthened them all and made them face their enemy in a peaceful way. The terrorists today lack any spiritual connection with God or with their community and instead are taken in by extremist propaganda.

Many terrorist groups claim they are fighting for a religious cause. This claim is nonsensical, as it is completely against all faiths or beliefs in God (or a spiritual being) to use terrorist violence. Many terrorists claim to be part of Islam, but nothing in Islam allows for a person to shoot or bomb innocent victims. Such murderous actions come from a psychotic mind, isolated from God and spiritually disconnected from humankind. Islam, Christianity, Buddhism, and many other faiths all predict this kind of evil will come from a lack of spirituality.

An illuminating example of a group of people who were spiritually disconnected and murderous but became spiritually connected and peaceful, involves a tribe of natives living in the jungles along the Amazon river. Russel T. Hitt describes the Waodani (Auca) Indians in his book, *Jungle Pilot*, as an isolated tribe that followed a practice of periodically raiding neighboring tribal villages and spearing to death as many opponents as possible. They had also killed early missionaries who tried to make contact. The book describes how a missionary pilot named Nate Saint managed to fly slowly over the Waodani's village and exchange messages so that he finally felt he could land and make contact in person. The first encounter went well, but on a subsequent encounter, the Waodani massacred Saint and the missionaries with him.

Nevertheless, the remaining missionaries did not give up, and they eventually made peaceful contact and brought the Christian message to the Waodani. Nate's son, Stephen Saint, also a missionary, eventually befriended the people who murdered his father, and they stayed lifelong friends as fellow Christians.[117] This incredible story shows that the power of God is immeasurable, and that the importance of spiritual connections should not be underestimated, even in the face of unspeakable evil or violence.

We may not feel as confident as these missionaries were in the face of evil. Nevertheless, we can seek out those who are lonely and show them compassion. We can start by reconciling with people with whom we have any disagreement, especially one that has led to estrangement. If all of us acted in this simple way, the results would be powerful. We do not need a major movement or government program to help us. We just need God's help and the support of one another.

Twelve

Our Great Commission

Building Spiritual Connections

We face many challenges to having a spiritual life and spiritual connections with God and with others. However, if we realize that God is all-powerful, then these challenges become surmountable with His help. The first step is to be introspective. How am I living my life now? What can I do in my own life to become more spiritual? In answering these questions, we can begin to seek a more spiritual life.

Concentrating on what we can control ourselves is part of the introspective process. Stephen Covey's first habit in *Seven Habits of Highly Effective People* is to "be proactive." He discusses the idea that all of us have "circles of influence" within which we can control things (primarily dealing with ourselves), and "circles of concern" within which we have things that concern us, but which we may or may not be able to control.[118] Other people's actions are typically beyond our control. Yet how many of us seek to change other people or fret over the actions of others? It is a waste of time. We should concentrate on our own selves and our own actions.

In the Sermon on the Mount Jesus teaches us to work on our own spirituality before trying to help or correct others:

> And why do you look at the speck in your brother's eye, but do not consider the plank in your own eye? Or how can you say to your brother, "Let me remove the speck from your eye;" and look, a plank is in your own eye? Hypocrite! First remove the plank from your own eye, and then you will see clearly to remove the speck from your brother's eye.[119]

His point is that judging the errors in others is fruitless while we harbor our own errors and ignore them. Therefore, the first step is to frankly assess our own spiritual state, then to seek a spiritual connection with God and those around us. Once we do this, then we can effectively begin to help others to become more spiritual. But how does one connect with God? Each faith has different approaches, but they all encourage prayer. How should one pray? Again, each faith differs in the details. However, all you really have to do is to clear your mind of its daily distractions and ask God to help you. God will show you how to pray, even if you do not know what to say. Just approaching God with the attitude that you need His help and guidance is all it takes to get started—the rest will happen naturally. As you connect with other spiritual people, see how they pray and relate to God. The Bible and other books of faith also give guidance on prayer. Fundamentally, true prayer is the heartfelt reaching out to God, and God will answer.

In our spiritual quest, we must not get caught up in the factional fighting and political causes against this or that, for none of these actions improve our spiritual connections. During the 2004 US presidential election, there was a billboard off a main highway that read *Vote the Bible*. The implied meaning was that voting for one of the candidates would be more "biblically sound" than voting for the other. But this message failed to consider that all presidential candidates are sinners, capable of many faults, just like all of the rest of us. The President of the United States may be a very successful, powerful person, but he or she is still human and still only as capable of doing right or wrong as anyone else. Hoping to improve the spiritual life of the country through political action is completely illogical and unbiblical.

Consider the first Christians in ancient Rome. The Roman government persecuted them mercilessly. Christians were routinely hunted down and pitted against wild beasts as entertainment in the coliseum. Roman society was pagan and largely immoral. Yet nowhere in Christ's teachings or in any subsequent teaching of his apostles is there any call to action against the Roman government. In fact, quite the opposite is taught. Jesus tells the Jewish Pharisees who ask whether or not they should pay the onerous taxes demanded by the Romans, to "give to Caesar what is Caesar's, and to God what is God's."[120] In other words, pay the tax to the Roman authorities, but keep one's connection with God. Peter also advises the believers of Christ to "honor the king," [121] or respect the governmental authority.

Instead, the call to action is for the believers in Christ to treat others with the same respect and love that they themselves desire. Jesus sums this up in His Sermon on the Mount. "Therefore, whatever you want men to do to you, do also to them, for this is the Law and the Prophets."[122] He is saying that all of the Scriptures up to that point guide us to behave charitably toward others, as we hope and wish for them to treat us charitably in turn. He even exhorts His followers to "love your enemies and pray for those who persecute you." [123] He expects us to spiritually connect with everyone, not just with those we like. The stronger we make our spiritual connections with one another, the stronger will be our spiritual connection with God.

The Bible and many other religious teachings warn us to avoid aspects of the world around us that hurt our spirituality. The apostle John says:

> Do not love the world or anything in the world. If anyone loves the world, the love of the Father is not in him. For everything in the world—the cravings of sinful man, the lust of his eyes and the boasting of what he has and does—comes not from the Father but from the world. The world and its desires pass away, but the man who does the will of God lives forever.[124]

In other words, we must not concentrate on finding satisfaction in life from the material world around us, but rather through the spiritual connection we form with God and with other people. Other religions have a similar message. Khurshid Ahmad states:

> That the present [world] order is characterized by injustice and exploitation is proved beyond any shadow of doubt. But Islam suggests that the present order fails because it is based upon a wrong concept of man and of his relationship with other human beings, with society, with nature, and with the world.[125]

Islam guides believers to connect with God and with one another. The current world with all its trends that hurt spirituality is failing, as it has become so unspiritual. Therefore, the believers of Islam must work to change it.

Zen Buddhists believes that all humans can connect spiritually with God if they clear their minds through meditation (*zazen*). Clearing the mind, ridding oneself of all the distractions of the world around us, or bad karma, is the goal of Zen. Bad karma is similar to the idea of sin, the spiritual disconnection caused by our own self-centered thoughts and behavior. Therefore, a Zen Buddhist seeks to rid himself or herself of bad karma and return to the original spiritual state, in harmony with God and all creation.[126] Likewise, Native American beliefs focus on achieving harmony with Mother Earth, or nature and all creation, in tune with the Great Spirit.[127]

In all cases, we must build spiritual connections with God's help. This requires us first to examine ourselves and ask truthfully what we hold to be most important in life. All of us need spiritual connections, and we must begin with a frank assessment on how well we have tried to build them. It is a personal quest and can only occur between each person and God. Acknowledging our need for a spiritual life is the first step in building connections with God and with others.

Bryan: It took me many years to understand this process of spiritual renewal, and I am still learning. My first, most important lesson, however, was in college. My freshman and sophomore years, I descended more and more into a self-centered pursuit of girls and parties. At the same time, my grades got worse and worse and I felt worse and worse. I remember walking back to my dorm room one night, completely depressed, alone, and empty in spirit. At the start of junior year, I made a conscious decision that I would change my actions, and I would only seek to go out with friends and seek to deepen those friendships. I also began to read the Bible for the first time. Everything improved, especially my outlook on life. Then, in my senior year, I felt the need to join a church, and through a friend, met a priest and ended up joining the Roman Catholic Church. I prayed and built a much stronger relationship with God and with those around me. I did not become a perfect person by any stretch, but I was much more content and peaceful. I realize now that what I had done was to build a spiritual connection with God and with others, and those connections saved me. *~End~*

Maggie: As a seventeen-year-old senior in high school, I feel that I am still very much a novice in the spiritual sense. I have been raised Catholic and have attended Sunday masses ever since I can remember. Despite this consistent attendance and my family's background, I've realized that I am not solely devoted to the Roman Catholic faith. Over the past couple of years, I have come to the conclusion that the religion one belongs to is of less importance than the individual's own faith and goodness. Love isn't specific to any language, culture, or religion; it is universal. I intend to explore different sects of Christianity and to find a church in which I feel closest to God.

Until I settle, I am content with focusing on my relationship with Him and my relationship with the people around me. I will strive to strengthen my faith and grow in my connections with others. *~End~*

A positive action we can take to help ourselves in this process is to serve others. Service is a manifestation of *agape* (spiritual love), as long as we serve with no expectation of reward or recognition. Jesus served many people that the Jewish community had ostracized, and in doing so, he not only gave up any hope of reward, but earned condemnation. He also served people personally and humbly, such as washing his disciples' feet before the Passover supper.[128]

Another positive action we can take is to forgive others, especially where long-standing disagreements occur. Again, from the Sermon on the Mount, "For if you forgive men their trespasses, your heavenly Father will also forgive you. But if you do not forgive men their trespasses, neither will your Father forgive your trespasses."[129] *Trespass* is another word for sin, or disobeying God by straying from His guidance. If God has not forgiven us, He will not connect with us, so we must seek forgiveness to connect spiritually. God will always forgive us, by the way, no matter what we have done—we just have to ask. Forgiving others is the first step, and as we reconcile ourselves to others, we also become reconciled to God. Stephen Saint's forgiveness of the Waodani tribe that had murdered his father is an extraordinary example to emulate.

Therefore, while we may take an interest in politics and vote a certain way, or speak out for a certain cause or against certain policies, we should not believe these actions will do anything for us or anyone else spiritually. Only by God's grace can we trust to spiritually connect with God and others. We can also work on keeping ourselves in a frame of mind and in an environment that is as conducive as possible to enable interpersonal spiritual connections. For example, we can forego many of the modern world's distractions and turmoil and instead be sociable and charitable toward others. If we follow Jesus's great commission "to go forth and make disciples of all nations"[130] then we focus on reaching out to others and helping them connect with God and one another. In the end, what we do ourselves in concert with God is what matters most in our quest for spirituality. As the Zen master, Deshimaru, explains:

> In Christianity Jesus sacrificed himself for everybody else and so he is still living. Religions teach that we should abandon the ego in order to help, to serve others; and that is exactly the hardest thing for a human being to do. Our modern civilization could hardly be more egotistical. And people are unhappy. Abandoning the ego is difficult, but it is necessary, in order to influence others.[131]

Conclusion

"The Lord is close to the broken hearted and saves those who are crushed in spirit."

Psalm 34:18 (Holy Bible, New International Version)

All faiths assert the central importance of spiritual connections in life. Peace, contentment, and benevolence all come from firm spiritual connections with others and with God. But in our modern world, many forces hurt or break these connections. As a result, we see widespread violence, discontent, and malevolence. Ironically, most public discussion on these problems ignores any spiritual aspect and seeks solutions in the same type of humanist and materialist policies that generated the problems in the first place.

For example, in response to school shootings, lawmakers have debated and passed new gun restrictions. Impartial experts indicate that the restrictions are generally useless, although they succeed in exacerbating the controversy between the pro- and anti-gun lobbies, furthering more spiritual disconnection between people. In the end, the spiritual state of the shooter is ignored, and the next shooter comes along and surprises everyone once again. While many survivors may seek spiritual connections for help and comfort, the general attitude in society is to overlook these connections and to seek another humanist or materialist solution.

While the preindustrial world was slower-paced and more traditional, it certainly had spiritual problems. Nevertheless, the modern world has many destructive aspects, hindering spiritual connections even more. The information society is a time of accelerated change, making it more and more difficult to meet and connect with those around us. It can make us too busy to think about God. Secular humanism emphasizes our individuality, making us less willing to submit to communal goals or a higher authority, as it treats individuals as gods. Materialism emphasizes the physical world around us and encourages us to seek pleasure in the world while denying God. Socialism emphasizes the power of the state to solve all our problems, so the state replaces God, family, and community in our lives. Globalization and urbanization both emphasize commerce over all other aspects of life, so we neglect God and human connections for the pursuit of wealth. In all cases, the average person is left feeling spiritually desolate.

In response, we need to examine ourselves and our own spirituality. Then, we can begin to build spiritual connections, both with God and with those around us. No government interference or encouragement is needed or wanted in this effort. No political action or social justice movement is warranted, either. It must be one person acting upon another, with God's help. All major faiths generally support this approach. In the end, spiritual connections will give us an inner peace and contentment with life, even in our unspiritual modern society, as David describes in his twenty-third Psalm:

> The Lord is my shepherd; I shall not want.
>
> He makes me lie down in green pastures;
>
> He leads me beside the still waters.
>
> He restores my soul;
>
> He leads me in the paths of righteousness for His name's sake.
>
> Yea, though I walk through the valley of the shadow of death, I will fear no evil;
>
> For You are with me;
>
> Your rod and Your staff, they comfort me.
>
> You prepare a table before me in the presence of my enemies; You anoint my head with oil;
>
> My cup runs over.
>
> Surely goodness and mercy shall follow me all the days of my life;
>
> And I will dwell in the house of the Lord forever.[132]

About the Authors

Bryan Holmes is a teacher, retired United States Air Force officer and pilot, and lifelong learner. He has been a Christian since his youth and studied the Bible extensively. He has a bachelor's degree in physics from the University of North Carolina at Chapel Hill, a master's degree in administration from Central Michigan University, a master's degree in liberal studies from Fort Hays State University, and a sixth year graduate degree in educational leadership from Southern Connecticut State University. He has lived in Italy, Japan, and England, for a total of over ten years overseas. He is married and has three children.

Maggie McSpedon is a high school senior with diverse interests and abilities. While looking at college programs in science and engineering, she is also pursuing her love of writing. She is a Christian and has served both in her church and on missions.

Bibliography

____. "A Short History of Enclosure in Britain." *The Land: An Occasional Magazine about Land Rights* (2009). Accessed 8/21/2013 from http://www.thelandmagazine.org.uk/articles/short-history-enclosure-britain.

____. *Constitution of the United States*. Washington, DC: Commission on the Bicentennial of the United States Constitution, 1989.

____. "Cultural Dimension of Globalization." *Trade, Foreign Policy, Diplomacy and Health*. World Health Organization, 2013. Accessed 8/21/2013 from http://www.who.int/trade/glossary/story012/en/index.html.

____. *Holy Bible: King James Version (KJV)*. Philadelphia: National Publishing Company, 1968. Used by permission. All rights reserved.

____. *Holy Bible: New International Version (NIV)*. Grand Rapids: Sondervan Publishing, 1973, 1978, 1984. Used by permission. All rights reserved.

____. *Holy Bible: New King James Version (NKJV)*. Nashville: Thomas Nelson, 1979, 1980, 1982. Used by permission. All rights reserved.

____. "Humanism." *New World Encyclopedia, 2008*. Accessed 8/19/2013 from http://www.newworldencyclopedia.org/entry/Humanism.

____. "In God we trust, maybe, but not each other." Associated Press / GFK poll, 2013. Accessed 12/3/2013 from http://ap-gfkpoll.com/featured/our-latest-poll-findings-24.

____. "Interview with Francis Collins." *Question of God*. Public Broadcasting Service (PBS): WGBH Educational Foundation, 2004. Accessed 7/11/2013 from http://www.pbs.org/wgbh/questionofgod/voices/collins.html.

____. *New Agriculture Policy*. Ministry of Information and Broadcasting, Government of India, 2013. Accessed 8/21/2013 from http://rrtd.nic.in/agriculture.html.

____. *Policy Manual on HEALTH CARE: Standards Regarding the Delivery of Health Care. Section 44-5-4, Termination of Pregnancy.* Department of Children and Families. State of Connecticut, 2007. Accessed 12/8/2013 from http://www.ct.gov/dcf/cwp/view.asp?a=2639&Q=395024.

____. *Recidivism.* State of Connecticut, Department of Correction, Office of Policy and Management, 2012. Accessed 8/19/2013 from http://www.ct.gov/ doc/cwp/view.asp?a=1492&Q=305970.

____. "The Mississippi Delta, Scratching a Living: A Shocking Rate of Depopulation in the Rural South." *The Economist* (June 8, 2013). Accessed 8/21/2013 from http://www.economist.com/news/united-states/21579025-shocking-rate-depopulation-rural-south-scratching-living.

____. *Understanding School Violence.* Center for Disease Control, Division of Adolescent and School Health, 2012. Accessed 8/24/2013 from http://www.cdc.gov/violenceprevention/pdf/schoolviolence_factsheet-a.pdf.

____. *Urbanization and Global Change.* Ann Arbor: University of Michigan, 2002. Accessed 8/21/2013 from http://www.globalchange.umich.edu/globalchange2/current/lectures/urban_gc/.

____. *Urbanization: A Majority in Cities.* United Nations Population Fund, 2007. Accessed 7/10/2013 from http://www.unfpa.org/pds/urbanization.htm.

____. *Welfare Reform: Ten Years Later.* Urban Institute, 2006. Accessed 7/10/2013 from http://www.urban.org/toolkit/issues/welfarereform.cfm.

____. "Where We Stand: Building the Next Left." Democratic Socialists of America. Posted 2/6/1998. Accessed 12/25/2013 from http://www.dsausa.org/where_we_stand.

Babayeva, Svetlana. "Free from Morality, Or What Russia Believes In Today." *Russia in Global Affairs* (August 8, 2007). Accessed 8/21/2013 from http://eng.globalaffairs.ru/number/n_9124.

Berry, Wendell. "It All Turns on Affection." *2012 Jefferson Lecture*. National Endowment for the Humanities. Accessed 8/21/2013 from http://www.neh.gov/about/awards/jefferson-lecture/wendell-e-berry-lecture.

Beston, Henry. *The Outermost House*. New York: Ballantine Books, 1928, revised 1949.

Brand, Chad, Charles Draper and Archie England, ed. *Holman Illustrated Bible Dictionary*. Nashville: Holman Bible Publishers, 2003.

Buck, Pearl S. *China As I See It*. New York: The John Day Company, 1970.

Capra, Fritjof. *The Hidden Connections*. New York: Random House, 2002.

Capra, Fritjof. *The Web of Life*. New York: Doubleday, 1996.

Castells, Manuel. "An Introduction to the Information Age" (1997). In *The Information Society Reader*. Edited by Frank Webster. London: Routledge, 2004.

Chhang, Youk and Northwestern University School of Law. "Historical Overview of the Khmer Rouge." *Cambodia Tribunal Monitor*. Northwestern University School of Law Center for International Human Rights and Documentation Center of Cambodia, 2013. Accessed 8/19/2013 from http://www.cambodiatribunal.org/history/khmer-rouge-history.

Covey, Stephen R. *The Seven Habits of Highly Effective People*. New York: Simon & Schuster, 1989.

Deshimaru, Taisen. *Questions to a Zen Master*. New York: E.P. Dutton, 1985.

Dimitri, Carolyn, Anne Effland, and Neilson Conklin. *The 20th Century Transformation of U.S. Agriculture and Farm Policy*. United States Department of Agriculture, Washington: Economic Research Service, 2005.

Dokoupil, Tony. "The Suicide Epidemic." *Newsweek* (May 22, 2013). Accessed 7/11/2013 from http://www.thedailybeast.com/newsweek/2013/05/22/why-suicide-has-become-and-epidemic-and-what-we-can-do-to-help.html.

Drucker, Peter. *Post-Capitalist Society*. New York: Harper Business, 1993.

Elkhamri, Mounir, Grau, Lester W., King-Irani, Laurie, Mitchell, Amanda S. and Tasa- Bennett, Lenny. "Urban Population Control in a Counterinsurgency." Fort Leavenworth: Foreign Military Studies Office. Accessed on 12/25/2013 from http://fmso.leavenworth.army.mil/documents/Urban-control.pdf.

Friedman, Thomas L. *Hot, Flat and Crowded*. New York: Farrar, Straus and Giroux, 2008.

Haisha, Lisa. "Is Your Facebook Addiction a Sign of Loneliness?" *Huffington Post* (April 3, 2010). Accessed 7/5/2013 from http://www.huffingtonpost.com/ lisa-haisha/is-your-facebook-addictio_b_533530.html.

Heyrman, Christine Leigh. "Native American Religion in Early America." *Divining America, TeacherServe®*. National Humanities Center, 2013. Accessed 7/8/2013 from http://nationalhumanitiescenter.org/tserve/ eighteen/ekeyinfo/natrel.htm.

Hitt, Russel T. *Jungle Pilot*. Grand Rapids: Discovery House Publishers, 1997.

Huang, Yasheng. *Capitalism with Chinese Characteristics: Entrepreneurship and the State*. New York: Cambridge University Press, 2008.

Joffe-Walt, Chana. "Unfit for Work: The Startling Rise of Disability in America." *Planet Money*. National Public Radio, 2013. Accessed 8/21/2013 from http://apps.npr.org/unfit-for-work/.

Kirk, Chris. "Since 1980, 297 People Have Been Killed in School Shootings. An Interactive Chart of Every School Shooting and Its Death Toll." *Slate Magazine* (2012). The Slate Group, A Division of the Washington Post Company. Accessed 8/24/2013 from http://www.slate.com/articles/news_and_politics/map_of_the_week/2012/12/sandy_hook_a_chart_of_all_196_fatal_school_shootings_since_1980_map.html.

Lasch, Christopher. "Degradation of the Practical Arts" (1987). In *The Information Society Reader*. Edited by Frank Webster. London: Routledge, 2004.

Lyon, David. "New Directions in Theory" (2001). In *The Information Society Reader*. Edited by Frank Webster . London: Routledge, 2004.

MacLeod, Calum. "China Orders Children to Visit Their Aging Parents." *USA Today*, July 1, 2013. Accessed on 12/25/2013 from http://www.usatoday.com/story/news/world/2013/07/01/china-children/2480593/.

Magoulick, Mary. *Native American Worldview Emerges*. Accessed 7/10/2013 from http://www.faculty.de.gcsu.edu/~mmagouli/worldview.htm.

Mam, Teeda Butt. "Worms from Our Skin." *Children of Cambodia's Killing Fields: Memoirs by Survivors*. Compiled by Dith Pran. New Haven: Yale University, 1997. Accessed 8/21/2013 from http://www.nytimes.com/books/first/p/pran-cambodia.html.

Mawdudi, Abulala. *Towards Understanding Islam (Eighth Edition)*. Edited and introduced by Khurshid Mawdudi (1979). Salimiah, Kuwait: International Islamic Federation of Student Organizations, 1986.

McDonald, Barry, Editor. *Seeing God Everywhere: Essays on Nature and the Sacred (Perennial Philosophy)*. Bloomington: World Wisdom, 2003.

Naimark, Norman. *Stalin's Genocides (Human Rights and Crimes Against Humanity)*. Princeton: Princeton University Press, 2011.

Norris, Pippa. "The Digital Divide" (2000). In *The Information Society Reader*. Edited by Frank Webster. London: Routledge, 2004.

Parker-Pope, Tara. "Suicide Rates Rise Sharply in U.S." *New York Times* (May 3, 2013). Accessed 7/11/2013 from http://www.nytimes.com/2013/05/03/ health/suicide-rate-rises-sharply-in-us.html?_r=0.

Putnam, Robert D. *Bowling Alone: The Collapse and Revival of American Community*. New York: Simon & Schuster, 2010.

Rackham, Oliver. *The Illustrated History of the Countryside*. London: Seven Dials, Cassell & Co, 1994.

Rector, Robert and Patrick F. Fagan. *The Continuing Good News About Welfare Reform*. The Heritage Foundation, 2003. Accessed 7/10/2013 from http:// www.heritage.org/research/reports/2003/02/the-continuing-good-news.

Robespierre, Maximilien. "Toward Authoritarian Collectivism?" (1793). In *Great Problems in European Civilization*. Edited by Kenneth M. Setton and Henry R. Winkler. Englewood Cliffs: Prentice-Hall, Inc. 1966.

Schweitzer, Albert. *Indian Thought and Its Development*. London: Hodder and Stoughton, Ltd., 1936.

Simone C., L. Carolin, S. Max S., and K. Reinhold. "Associations between Community Characteristics and Psychiatric Admissions in an Urban Area." *Social Psychiatry Psychiatric Epidemiology* (March 5, 2013). Accessed 7/10/2013 from http://www.ncbi.nlm.nih.gov/pubmed/23460045.

Smith, Adam. *The Wealth of Nations*. London: George Routledge and Sons, 1893.

Stevenson, Betsey and Justin Wolfers. "The Paradox of Declining Female Happiness." *NBER Working Paper No. 14969*. National Bureau of Economic Research, 2009. Accessed 7/10/2013 from http://www.nber.org/ papers/w14969.

Strong, James H. *Strong's Exhaustive Concordance (Compact Edition)*. Grand Rapids: Baker Book House, 1997.

Urry, John. "Is Britain the First Post-Industrial Society?" (1995). In *The Information Society Reader*. Edited by Frank Webster. London: Routledge, 2004.

Webster, Frank. "Introduction: Information Society Studies." In *The Information Society Reader*. Edited by Frank Webster. London: Routledge, 2004.

Yeung, Yue-man. "Globalization and the New Urban Challenge." *Keynote Address for the South Asia Urban and City Management Course, World Bank Institute* (2000). Accessed 8/21/2013 from http://info.worldbank.org/ etools/docs/library/110657/ goa/assets/g-yeung-modoo.pdf.

Yi, Pu. *From Emperor to Citizen: The Autobiography of Aisin-Gioro Pu Yi.* Oxford: Oxford University Press, 1987.

Notes

1 Schweitzer, *Indian Thought and Its Development*, vi.
2 Webster, *The Information Society Reader*, 1.
3 Capra, *The Web of Life*, 30.
4 See Capra, *The Hidden Connections*, 67.
5 Capra, *The Hidden Connections*, 68.
6 McDonald, *Serving God Everywhere*, xxi.
7 Beston, *The Outermost House*, 8.
8 *NIV*, Psalm 19:1.
9 *NIV*, Romans 1:20
10 See *NKJV*, Genesis 1 and 2.
11 See *NKJV*, Genesis 3.
12 *NKJV*, Romans 5:12.
13 *NIV*, Romans: 1:21-23, 28
14 *NIV*, Genesis 4:26.
15 *NKJV*, Leviticus 19:18.
16 *NKJV*, Deuteronomy 6:5.
17 See Strong, *Exhaustive Concordance*.
18 *NKJV*, Luke 10:25-28.
19 See Strong, *Exhaustive Concordance*.
20 *NKJV*, John 3:16.
21 *NKJV*, John 15:1-2,4-5.
22 *NKJV*, John 15:10.
23 *NIV*, Psalm 19:7.
24 See *NKJV*, Luke 15:11-32.
25 See *Policy Manual on Health Care*, Connecticut Department of Children and Families.
26 *NIV*, Exodus 20:12.
27 *KJV*, Matthew 19:19.
28 *NKJV*, Luke 10:29.
29 See *NKJV*, Luke 10:30-37.
30 Associated Press poll.
31 *NKJV*, Matthew 5:7.
32 *NKJV*, Matthew 5:23-24.
33 *NKJV*, 1 Corinthians 13:13.
34 *NKJV*, Acts 4:32.
35 *NKJV*, Luke 16:26.
36 *NKJV*, Phillipians 4:6-7.
37 Mawdudi, *Towards Understanding Islam*, 11.
38 Ibid., 11.
39 Ibid., 25.

---

40 Ibid., 29.
41 Ibid., 105.
42 Ibid., see 36.
43 Deshimaru, *Questions to a Zen Master*, 4.
44 Ibid., 13.
45 Ibid., 13.
46 Ibid., 27-28.
47 Ibid., 30.
48 See Heyrman, "Native American Religion in Early America."
49 Ibid.
50 Rackham, *The Illustrated History of the Countryside*, 193-194.
51 Dimitri, Effland, and Conklin, *Transformation of US Agriculture*, 29.
52 Drucker, *Post-Capitalist Society*, 31.
53 Webster, *The Information Society Reader*, 1.
54 Urry, "Is Britain the First Post-Industrial Society?" 126.
55 See Ibid., 131.
56 Castells, "An Introduction to the Information Age," 142.
57 Ibid., 143.
58 Drucker, *Post-Capitalist Society*, 60.
59 Haisha, "Is Your Facebook Addiction a Sign of Loneliness?"
60 See Norris, "The Digital Divide," 273.
61 See Lyon, "New Directions in Theory," 329-333.
62 See Drucker, *Post-Capitalist Society*, 168.
63 Ibid., 174.
64 *NKJV*, Romans 8:38-39.
65 *Constitution of the United States.*
66 See "Humanism," *New World Encyclopedia.*
67 *NIV*, Proverbs 14:12.
68 State of Connecticut, Department of Correction.
69 See Robespierre, "Toward Authoritarian Collectivism?"
70 See Chhang, "Historical Overview of the Khmer Rouge."
71 Ibid.
72 *NKJV*, 1 Peter 1:24-25.
73 "Interview with Francis Collins," PBS.
74 *NKJV*, Ecclesiastes 2:10-11.
75 *NKJV*, Matthew 19:23-24.
76 *NKJV*, Matthew 6:19-21.
77 *NKJV*, 1 Timothy 6:17.
78 Democratic Socialists of America website.
79 Babayeva, "Free from Morality, or What Russia Believes in Today."
80 Smith, *The Wealth of Nations*, 298.
81 See Naimark, *Stalin's Genocides.*
82 See Yi, *From Emperor to Citizen.*

[83] See Rector and Fagan, *The Continuing Good News about Welfare Reform* and *Welfare Reform: Ten Years Later*, Urban Institute.
[84] *NKJV*, Matthew 5:44.
[85] Mam, "Worms from Our Skin."
[86] See Buck, *China as I See It*, 25-26.
[87] *USA Today*, July 1, 2013.
[88] Friedman, *Hot, Flat and Crowded*, 29-30.
[89] "Cultural Dimensions of Globalization," World Health Organization.
[90] Lasch, "Degradation of the Practical Arts," 291.
[91] Capra, *The Hidden Connections*, 144.
[92] *Urbanization: A Majority in Cities*, United Nations Population Fund.
[93] Yeung, "Globalization and the New Urban Challenge," 4.
[94] "A Short History of Enclosure in Britain," *The Land*.
[95] "The Mississippi Delta, Scratching a Living," *The Economist*.
[96] See *Urbanization and Global Change*, University of Michigan.
[97] *New Agriculture Policy*, Ministry of Information and Broadcasting, Government of India (2013).
[98] Berry, "It All Turns on Affection."
[99] Elkhamri et al., "Urban Population Control in a Counterinsurgency," 1.
[100] See Huang, *Capitalism with Chinese Characteristics*, 109-112.
[101] Simone et al., "Associations between Community Characteristics and Psychiatric Admissions."
[102] Stevenson and Wolfers, "The Paradox of Declining Female Happiness," 5-6.
[103] See Parker-Pope, "Suicide Rates Rise Sharply in US."
[104] Ibid.
[105] Ibid.
[106] *NKJV*, Ecclesiastes 1:14.
[107] See Dokoupil, "The Suicide Epidemic."
[108] See Ibid.
[109] See Putnam, *Bowling Alone*.
[110] Kirk, "School Shootings."
[111] See *Understanding School Violence*, Center for Disease Control.
[112] *NKJV*, Genesis 6:11.
[113] See Strong, *Exhaustive Concordance*.
[114] *NKJV*, Proverbs 4:17.
[115] *NKJV*, Ezekiel, 8:17.
[116] Brand et al., ed., *Holman Illustrated Bible Dictionary*, 1652.
[117] See Hitt, *Jungle Pilot*.
[118] See Covey, *Seven Habits of Highly Successful People*, 81-86.
[119] *NKJV*, Matthew 7:3-5.
[120] *NIV*, Matthew 22:21.
[121] *NKJV*, 1 Peter 2:17.
[122] *NKJV*, Matthew 7:12.

[123] *NIV*, Matthew 5:44.
[124] *NIV*, 1 John 2:15-17.
[125] Mawdudi, *Towards Understanding Islam*, 14.
[126] See Deshimaru, *Questions to a Zen Master*, 5-7.
[127] See Magoulick, *Native American Worldview Emerges*.
[128] See *NKJV*, John 13.
[129] *NKJV*, Matthew 6:14-15.
[130] See *NIV*, Matthew 28: 16-20.
[131] Deshimaru, *Questions to a Zen Master*, 16.
[132] NKJV, Psalm 23.

CPSIA information can be obtained at www.ICGtesting.com
Printed in the USA
BVOW11s1852260814

364346BV00013B/448/P